DOORBELLS, DA
AND DEAD BAT
USER RESEARCH WAR STORIES

Steve Portigal

Rosenfeld Media
Brooklyn, New York

Doorbells, Danger, and Dead Batteries
User Research War Stories
By Steve Portigal

Rosenfeld Media, LLC

457 Third Street, #4R

Brooklyn, New York

11215 USA

On the Web: www.rosenfeldmedia.com

Please send errors to: errata@rosenfeldmedia.com

Publisher: Louis Rosenfeld

Managing Editor: Marta Justak

Interior Layout Tech: Danielle Foster

Cover Design: The Heads of State

Indexer: Marilyn Augst

Proofreader: Sue Boshers

ISBN: 1-933820-34-9

ISBN-13: 978-1-933820-34-7

LCCN: 2016955132

Printed and bound in the United States of America

This book is dedicated to Anne, Sharna, Cheryl, Bruce, Talia, and Arianna who fill my life with a bounty of story-worthy experiences.

HOW TO USE THIS BOOK

Who Should Read This Book?

The stories in this book will appeal broadly, but the lessons these stories offer are most valuable to people in the world of product development who spend time talking to users. Researchers, designers, product managers, software developers, marketers and beyond—anyone who is learning from people in order to do a better job at creating a thing should read this book. While someone with more experience interviewing users will likely see more connections to their own experience, the lessons here for doing better research are valuable to anyone who does—or will do—user research.

What's in This Book?

Each chapter deals with one challenging aspect of user research. A chapter begins with an overview of the topic and is then illustrated by several different war stories by different authors. The chapter concludes with a list of takeaways that show you how to apply the lessons of the stories to your own user research practice.

What Comes with This Book?

This book's companion website (http://rosenfeldmedia.com/books/user-research-war-stories/) contains a blog and additional content. The book's photos are available under a Creative Commons license (when possible) for you to download and include in your own presentations. You can find these on Flickr at www.flickr.com/photos/rosenfeldmedia/sets/.

FREQUENTLY ASKED QUESTIONS

What are war stories?

War stories are personal accounts of the challenges researchers have out in the field, where mishaps inevitably occur. The term originated around 1839 and is used broadly to describe the types of stories shared across many professions and communities, not just warriors and user researchers.

Why is this book about user research that went wrong?

There is a lot of material about the right way to do user research. But, in reality, sometimes things do go wrong (or to be precise, differently than intended). There's a lot to be learned from what actually happens, warts-and-all. With this insight, you might be able to prevent something unwanted from happening in the future, or at least have a better way of dealing with it the next time it comes up.

Should I read this book in one sitting?

While there are a lot of stories here, they are mostly pretty short, so you could binge-read them if you chose, but it's probably better to take it one chapter at a time. This gives you the opportunity to digest and reflect before diving in again.

Are there more stories?

Yes. The original archive is at www.portigal.com/category/series /warstories, and it includes stories that aren't in this book. As people contribute new stories, they'll be posted at that link, and at this book's companion website (http://rosenfeldmedia.com/books /user-research-war-stories/).

Can I submit my own story?

Yes, please! You can email story pitches to WarStories@portigal.com. Remember, these are stories about fieldwork (not about focus groups or usability tests). These stories are not about your research findings, but rather the kind of experiences that you have. Stories don't need to include company or client names.

CONTENTS

FOREWORD

We all *love* war stories. We love their two axiomatic narrative arcs: the protagonist having it all, losing it all, and then getting some of it back, along with a pile of redemption. We love the protagonist who has nothing, quests for something, finds it, and then invariably realizes that she or he was better off at the beginning. In fiction, these plots are predictable, but in real life, much less so. In real life, the "tale" is a precipitate that forms over time ... precisely through its retelling.

In this book, *Doorbells, Danger, and Dead Batteries: User Research War Stories,* Steve Portigal assembles an impressive platoon of these tales. But Steve is also an expert observer—indeed he does this for a living—so his gift in organizing and pulling out common threads throughout the book helps the reader make sense of these stories. Each section is bookended with an incredibly wise setup and useful takeaway, but he also provides permission for some dangling threads—acknowledging the temptation to slap a pretty bow on every anecdote. Rather, he provides permission to be okay with some lack of resolution.

War stories, as stories, contain all the usual tropes we see in good stories, but these stories are authentically unpredictable. And it's only in hindsight that they earn their stripes—to keep the metaphor—to be recounted, reexamined, and retold.

There are other military metaphors to explore as well. I personally have a hard time reconciling the notion of "rules of engagement" in the actual war arena, but certainly in the world of design that forms the scaffolding for the stories in this book, there are very *clear* rules of "design" engagement. Design research, user research, ethnography—these are all pretty mature disciplines at this point, with prescribed methods, best practices, and a more-or-less-agreed-upon moral code for working with human subjects. When things go wrong in *this* arena, well, they can go very wrong indeed.

There's also the "badge of honor" that people with war stories earn. They'd argue that you have to go through something to earn the medal (versus going around or over it), and they'd be right. Triumphing over adversity, or handling yourself gracefully when things go wrong, or just improvising in the moment can be hugely satisfying. In fact, it's in the retelling of the war story where the ultimate satisfaction (and sometimes the revenge!) actually lies. Like any retelling of a story, it usually gets better with age: the pacing improves, the extraneous details get excised as the critical ones sharpen up, and the whole thing just gets polished until the war story itself becomes a kind of crafted object. And abstracted from the event that birthed it, the story itself becomes more powerful. And worthy of collecting.

So we are grateful to Steve Portigal for assembling such a rich breadth of tales in his book. Throughout, he talks about the power of these stories—to instruct, to serve as catharsis, to entertain, to inspire. This book certainly delivers on all of these. It's hysterical, it's heartbreaking, and in the end it's, well, a triumph. And that's how wars are supposed to end, right?

—Allan Chochinov
Founding Chair, SVA MFA Products of Design
Partner, Core77

INTRODUCTION

> "We're wired for story. In a culture of scarcity and perfectionism, there's a surprisingly simple reason we want to own, integrate, and share our stories of struggle. We do this because we feel the most alive when we're connecting with others and being brave with our stories—it's in our biology."
>
> —Brené Brown, *Rising Strong*

I vividly remember the first time I sat at a hotel bar during a conference and swapped stories about the bizarre, hilarious, and daunting things that had happened out in the field doing research. It felt good to discover that we all had had similarly extreme experiences. Joyfully, I realized that I was actually part of a community of practice. These outlier stories facilitated my sense of belonging, as much, if not more, than the "real stuff" we were supposed to be getting out of fieldwork. I didn't realize it at the time, but we were sharing *war stories*.

A *war story* is a specific type of story: a personal story about how the storyteller encountered a challenge. Unlike other forms of storytelling, where you are inspired by how the storyteller overcame a challenge, in war stories, the storyteller doesn't necessarily prevail.

Over the past few years, I've been gathering and publishing war stories by other user researchers.[1] These stories show how research can actually be an exciting activity that is interpersonal, intimate, and unpredictable, even though it is often hard work. Let's face it—even experienced people may find themselves in situations they aren't prepared to deal with.

These stories are tremendously valuable. By reading these stories, we can learn from what went wrong for someone else (or at least what was different than expected). By sharing these stories, we can create an opportunity for researchers to reflect more deeply on what really happens in the field. This is a way to move beyond merely sharing "best practices" on the tactics of research (where every online forum for

---

1 http://www.portigal.com/category/series/warstories/

researchers has a regular posting asking about video camera models and online transcription services) to addressing the personal qualities that researchers work on bolstering their entire lives. There are no tactical solutions for most of the challenges encountered in war stories. Sometimes a solution isn't necessary or even appropriate. Rather, there are things that can be learned only when things go awry.

Some people approach their own skill development in user research in terms of *other people*. I am frequently asked questions like "How do I get a reluctant respondent to talk more?" and "How do I shut down a chatty participant?" These war stories show how much of doing research well is about what is within *us*. Improving our research skills, at least in part, is about coming to grips with our own flawed humanity.

Survivorship bias (also known as *winner's bias*) is a cognitive bias that manifests as a focus on the people or things that "survived" some process, while overlooking those that did not. Sometimes this is because what didn't survive just isn't visible. Survivorship bias leads to overly optimistic beliefs about how the world works, because it means we don't include the complete set of data, including both successes *and* failure. This type of thinking can lead to a false belief that a particular set of successes has some special property, rather than just coincidence. Culturally, our mindset encourages us to examine and emulate success in order to be successful ourselves. The prevalence of memoirs/profiles of successful business leaders is an artifact of that mindset.

Engineering and medicine have formally incorporated failure analysis into their practices, but in design, user experience, research, and so on, we don't have the appetite. Indeed, the reward structure in the cultures that many of us work in encourages (over)confident success stories, rather than humility and reflection, which ironically are the very qualities that make for successful researchers. The demand for clear and actionable insights means we may set aside these other stories, as they aren't "valuable."

In these stories, you'll see that research isn't a method executed on subjects; rather, it's an experience that people have together. Crucially, if more elusively, these stories reveal the priceless data that comes out of being in the field, the elements that aren't "findings," but are the ways in which we are personally—and permanently—changed. And you can't be changed this way while sitting at your desk, peering into your webcam at a research participant far, far away. When you step outside of your comfort zone, you are heading off to war, in a small but meaningful way. You are facing two stages of risk—the first from whatever unknown awaits you out there, and the second from the likelihood that you will return from the war forever changed.

With all the hype around reducing the effort to conduct research so that it fits more comfortably with other aspects of product development, we risk marginalizing research as a tool for validating decisions rather than as a strategic approach for understanding the world in a profoundly different way. The journey to reach that level of understanding is founded upon those experiences that change us, even if only in small ways. Risk be damned, being changed is integral to the work we seek to do. Uncovering a new way of looking at the world, of understanding the beliefs and desires of a group of people represents a change in ourselves. Being changed, we advocate for that understanding, exhorting and cajoling others to grasp the nuances of that understanding, so that they can bring new things into the world that will better support others. In risking being changed, we are changed. And so we try to change others, and we try to make something that changes the world for some.

These stories are artifacts. They are a representation of the essence of an experience. How you receive these stories will vary. You may feel empathy for the author, thinking about how awful, or how amazing their experience was. You may feel surprised that they failed to prepare for a challenging situation, or that they were bothered by something you would simply shrug off. You might think about what you would do in that situation, and how you would have made different choices. You might feel critical of what they did or in how they

This is the sort of question I'm utterly unprepared for. In this interview, I knew it was coming, some part of my body was tense from the discussion of the rationale for home schooling, knowing that I was in a slightly vulnerable situation that was going to emerge at some point. So, while I was dreading it all along, perhaps it came as some kind of relief. Watching the video later, I saw the most deadpan version of myself I'd ever seen: "Well ... perhaps that's a question for another time."

I was stuck. I couldn't dishonor all the rapport-building and honest curiosity I'd been exhibiting for the past two hours, but now we were trapped. My colleague spluttered helplessly in an endless loop of reflecting back what Jon had said previously. I kept waiting for my opening for the "Well, time to go," but Jon really wanted to talk to us about what we should be doing and thinking, with respect to Christ. It seems as if this went on for a very long time, but we finally made it to the doorway. Jon asked us to wait, and went off to get something. We should have made a break for it, but we were too ensnared by the requirements of politeness in our researcher role. He returned with some Bible-related literature and exhorted us intensely to follow up. Another eternity (if you will), and we were finally able to step away.

We made it to the car, drove a block, and erupted in hysterical, gasping laughter. It was the laughter of relief, the kind of manic giggling you'd get from 10-year-olds who just got away from the angry shopkeeper. We had some choice words about Jon, once we were safe.

The experience was terribly uncomfortable. I could not find a way to follow my own values as a researcher and still protect myself from a conversation that was personally risky. As a researcher, I was interested in and had respect for Jon's views on his family, his home, education, and the afterlife. But I really didn't want to have to reveal my own beliefs or defend them, especially in this setting.

The Best Laid Plans

Photo by Steve Portigal

*S*emper *Gumby* is an unofficial motto for the United States Marine Corps (and other military services). Adopted at a grassroots level, it references the official motto *Semper Fidelis* (Always Faithful), while invoking the built-in flexibility of that green clay character. It declares that successful military personnel must adapt to changes.

Some user researchers try to manage the complexity of research by crafting detailed plans and developing artifacts to support the act of planning, such as checklists, observation worksheets,[1] special notebooks for note-taking, and what's-in-your-bag fieldwork kits.[2] I put together my own set of re-purposable documents[3] to supplement *Interviewing Users*.

Planning, of course, is essential to successful fieldwork. And these artifacts can facilitate planning. But they can also imply, by their existence, if not their design, that things are going to go a certain way. Does the plan set you up to adapt, or are you in trouble when there's a snafu?[4] Sometimes these plans imply a simplicity to research, which may be more about selling the idea of research than actually empowering people to deal with the realities. Researchers learn—typically after losing some data—to bring extra batteries, to remind themselves to start the recording gear, to double-check they've brought along incentives and releases and interview guides and prototypes, and so on. But as these stories remind us, there's no complete set of circumstances that can be fully planned for. Should Dan Soltzberg (from his story in Chapter 9, "People Taking Care of People") have brought an extra pair of pants with him? There is no plan that can fully allow for the range of circumstances that can (and will) arise in and around fieldwork.[5] Semper Gumby, indeed.

So you have to plan. And yet planning can never be sufficient and even worse may lull you into a state of blithe overconfidence. Instead, think about the total experience of fieldwork as a system, or "a set of elements or parts that is coherently organized and interconnected in a pattern or structure that produces a characteristic set of behaviors."[6]

---

1 IDEO assembled a complete set of fieldwork documents: http://rfld.me/HCDGu

2 For example, Nick Bowmast's kit: http://rfld.me/EthKit

3 http://rosenfeldmedia.com/books/interviewing-users/#resources

4 A telling World War II–era acronym for "Situation Normal, All Fucked Up"

5 With apologies to Gödel and his Incompleteness Theorem

6 *Thinking in Systems: A Primer* by Donella H. Meadows

Typically, you use systems thinking when you consider your research data and when you design solutions, but what about the actual experience of doing fieldwork? It's a complex system. Thinking about the interconnectedness between different elements will help you anticipate some points of failure (bring more than enough batteries), but it should also help you accept that failures of some form or another are inevitable (but don't bring extra pants) and sometimes lead to other failures (a phenomenon known as *cascading failure*).

> **NOTE** EVERYBODY NEEDS TO PLAN
>
> I led a training workshop for a group of junior user researchers. I recommended using the field guide as a place to hold a number of critical process reminders (e.g., turn on the recording devices, sign the release form, etc.). One of the students reported, erroneously, to her boss, with an eye-roll and sigh, "He's telling us to turn on the camera." Her boss, a highly seasoned researcher, unaware of the higher order point I was attempting to teach, reminded her, "I've been doing this work for a long time, and I *still* forget to turn on the camera."

In this chapter, Julia Thompson, Tamara Christensen, and Jenn Downs experience cascading failures. Alicia Dornadic and her team try—and fail—to plan for the most basic of human needs. Dan Szuc and Mary Ann Sprague find that a small mistake has significant consequences, and they each explore how to adapt. Sean Ryan fails to plan adequately, and he works in blissful ignorance without consequence and only realizes later that he might have taken a different approach. George Ressler anticipates a point of failure and designs his approach to prevent that, but still must adapt on the fly. Each of these researchers, flawed human beings all, negotiate the slippery, shifting balance between intentionality and flexibility.

Julia Thompson: For Want of a Shoe

It all started with a simple question from the dispatcher: "Do you want a call when your taxi arrives?" My nonchalant answer, "No thanks, I should be OK," was the nail in my coffin. This was my first error in a series of cascading mistakes.

The next morning, I was heading out-of-country for in-home interviews. That night, in an effort to be as prepared as possible, I called to arrange a taxi for an early morning pickup. I hung up the phone and proceeded to pack my bags. I considered carefully what to pack. I visualized my next few days: What would the weather be like? What would be my mode of transportation? What clothing would be appropriate for the work—casual enough to fit into a home environment and dressy enough to fit into an office environment? I was sure that I had considered all the details. Unfortunately, the most important detail, my alarm, was what I missed.

Satisfied with my preparation, I went to bed and slept well. The next morning I awoke feeling refreshed. With birds chirping outside, sunlight filled the room. Yet something felt terribly wrong. What time was it? Why was it so light out? I picked up my phone, checked my alarm, and then checked the time. My stomach fell to the floor. My flight was leaving *now*.

Sheer panic overtook me. I couldn't think straight. I had never missed a flight before. I felt like I was going to throw up. I was paralyzed. I had no idea what to do. I grabbed my phone and called our corporate travel agent. It felt like hours as I waited on hold to ask my pressing questions: Could I still make my interview? When was the next flight? Could I fly out of a different airport instead? The sound of my heartbeat drowned out every noise as I sat there waiting, palms sweating, phone clutched. The agent came back on the line and said there was a flight leaving from another airport in two hours. Could I make it there in time? It's almost rush hour. It's an hour's drive with no traffic. What about parking? Customs? Security? If I took the car, how would my husband get to work? On top of all that, the agent still wasn't sure whether there was room on the flight.

We decided, together, that I should start driving, and I should stay on the line while she called the airline to confirm availability. I jumped in the car, with my phone on the passenger seat and that awful music taunting me as I continued to wait, on hold. I got about 10 minutes down the road when the agent told me to pull over and go home. That flight wouldn't be mine. I would settle for another flight, hours later, and hours after my scheduled interview.

Later that day, as my plane came in for its landing, I just felt low. I was tired from the emotional rollercoaster of missing my flight, I was anxious knowing I'd have to tell the people I was working with what had happened, and I was sad that I had missed out on an interview and the opportunity to see firsthand into the life of one of our customers. The only thing saving me was the fact that I was the client, so even though I missed the interview, it still went ahead as scheduled.

The following day I awoke in the right place and at the right time, with a better perspective on life. Our local research partner was gracious enough to include me in an interview that day. I was thankful. I was relieved. But now, that meant there would be four of us attending this interview. Two consultants and two clients: two too many. The consultant had called ahead and confirmed with our interviewee that it would be OK if an additional person (me!) attended the interview. Our interviewee was very accommodating and agreed to have all four of us into her home. I was so preoccupied with resolving my own error that I didn't consider, until later, how the dynamic of the interview would now be affected.

We all got to the interview, we all walked in, and we all sat down in the chairs offered to us by our interviewee. As everyone was setting up, I started to look around and take note of the environment. I noticed several pairs of shoes neatly arranged by the front door. I looked over at our host, I looked down: bare feet. My eyes darted around the room. I looked down at all our feet. *All four of us* had our shoes on, laces tied. *Bah!* We were the worst guests ever. Weren't we all, as researchers, supposed to notice something so simple but so important?

PHOTO BY JULIA THOMPSON

I spent the next five minutes cursing myself, my missed flight, the totally wrong and overpowering dynamic of four researchers to one customer, and the miss on basic shoe etiquette. I had to shake it off— all the feelings of shame, all the feelings of doubt—and I had to focus. I had to be in the moment. I had to get the most I could out of the interview, and I had to show the interviewee the respect she deserved.

It ended up being a great discussion. It was, by no means, a textbook in-context interview, but we had a nice dynamic emerge nonetheless. My story is not one of a single epic fail, but instead of a series of errors with a cascading effect. *"For want of a nail the shoe was lost, for want of a shoe the horse was lost … "* Here, we had not *for want of a shoe*, we had too many.

Alicia Dornadic: Don't Hate on a Tinkler

Going to someone's home for the first time to interview that person, especially in an unfamiliar culture and language, can be awkward. Showing up with two researchers, a cameraman, and a couple of clients in tow—all of whom are overcaffeinated and in need of a bathroom break—can make for a circus act. These were three-hour-long interviews, too. So, despite our best efforts to arrange feeding and peeing times before getting to the person's home, we usually all had to pee at some point during the interview.

But our translator was the absolute queen of tinkling. The first day I was understanding. "Maybe she's sick or nervous," I thought. She would take two to four breaks during each interview, which left the rest of us smiling and pointing at things dumbly, trying to make conversation in her absence. By the end of the week, my patience was shot. I was ready to strap some adult diapers on her. I would glower at her every time she asked for water, tea, or a soda. "Really?" I thought, my eyes on fire, "Should you really be having that?" I'm not proud of this. But I couldn't help being annoyed.

Finally, karma came to bite me on the ass. It was at the end of a long interview at the end of a long day, and I broke down and asked if I could use the restroom. Our host pointed to it, and I stumbled inside, missing the two-inch step down into it. There wasn't a lot of light in the bathroom, and it was cluttered. I couldn't find a switch. But no matter. I go. I reach for the toilet paper, and BOOM! CRASH! I take down the entire metal toilet paper rack off the wall, and it crashes onto the tiled floor. It was too dark to see how to fix it, so I had to come out and explain what I had done and apologize. Not only that, but my explanation and apology had to be translated! Translated and explained to two researchers, a cameraman, a couple of clients, and our participant. It ended up not being a big deal, but I was embarrassed. And I felt guilty for all my negative thoughts toward our translator. As much as I was annoyed at our tinkler friend, at least she didn't break anything.

Dan Szuc: Shanghai Surprise

We were on the train in Shanghai on our way to visit a person in their home as part of a research project. Doing random checks of all equipment becomes second nature, ensuring that you have backups of backups, cables work correctly, sound is being recorded correctly, and video is working well.

"LE MÉTRO DE SHANGHAI" (CC BY-ND 2.0) BY CHRISTIAN MANGE

We all have specific roles on home visits. Hok and I capture both the interview and surrounds on film using Flip cameras, Jo is responsible for speaking with the person we are visiting to ensure that they are comfortable, and Hok also is our guy for ensuring that all the equipment is technically working well (and if something is *not* working well, he usually knows how to fix it).

So back to the train ride in Shanghai ... the three of us were together, testing the recorder, cable, and microphone. We realized after conducting a few test recordings that there were clear breaks in the recording when playing it back. During the previous interview, we had gone through a security scanner at a train station with the participant (as part of the journey we were filming). The cable connecting the recorder and the bag were stretched going through security unnecessarily, possibly causing damage to the wires.

We tested various places where we thought the sound might be breaking up—the connectors, the microphone, and the cable itself. We wanted to get this right because the microphone clips onto the person we are interviewing and ensures that we have clear audio (in addition to the audio that's captured on the video using the Flip cameras). We did not have time to go to an electronics store to get new equipment and were relieved that the audio recorder itself was working well and could serve as a (non-ideal) backup microphone.

Together, we needed to come up with a plan to ensure that we could capture the same level and quality of audio as in the other people's stories captured to date in Shanghai. Consistent film quality is an important part of the storytelling. We tried a few configurations using the cables, rubber bands, and microphone. We eventually worked out a way to place the microphone close enough to the participant's chin so that the audio would come through clearly, and we discarded the faulty cable.

On reflection, it taught us all the importance of teamwork, thinking quickly about solutions, not blaming anyone when things sometimes go wrong, trying out various configurations while on the move, and planning ahead to have some other cables/equipment available if there were failures. Not everything goes according to plan in field research, but having a calm head and a team who works together makes for a nicer working environment and a huge difference in the overall results. Happy researchers lead to happy participants, which lead to nice stories and lots to learn from.

Sean Ryan: Pockets Full of Cash

It was back in my early days as an ethnographer. I was still a young pup in the field, doing consulting projects. I was teamed up with an elder anthropologist—a Puerto Rican woman who lived in Guadalajara, named Luz. We were doing a project for a major pharmaceutical

company that had just had great success with a new oral care product, so they thought they would try an ethnographic exploration
to uncover any other unmet needs. I think their aspirations at the
time were something like "We want the next $500 million consumer
product!" Luz and I were going to visit two field sites in Mexico:
Guadalajara and Tijuana. Living in Los Angeles, I was relatively
close to the border, and it wasn't yet seen as that dangerous to go to
Tijuana (i.e., no Mexican mafia drug lord street battles ... at least you
didn't read about them in the papers everyday). But I still had my
reservations, not possessing any Spanish language skills (outside of
the slang I had picked up from bartending in a Mexican restaurant
in Long Beach).

Having only been to Tijuana once to explore the finer points of
Avenida Revolución[7] (read: drinking tequila shots with college
kids and having my head shaken back and forth by a woman with
a whistle[8]), I had no real frame of reference for doing fieldwork in
TJ. As I quickly learned, neither did my counterpart Luz. She had
some relatives in TJ, but had never done fieldwork there. And so we
made what we later realized was a critical error in not pre-recruiting
participants before we went into the field. Upon arriving in Tijuana,
we quickly found ourselves literally approaching people in the
streets, in shops, etc., to ask about their oral care routines (a strange
encounter for the locals I'm sure). While this has all the hallmarks
of classic guerrilla recruiting it's never a comfortable situation to be
in, especially in a foreign country. Luz was doing her best to recruit
people while I stood by idly awaiting our field day fate.

Eventually, we started to have some success ... or so we thought.
One woman who worked in a nice department store in downtown TJ
offered to let us come to her home after work. We got her contact info
and told her we would see her that evening. We were offering $150 in
U.S. cash (this was more than 10 years ago) to interview participants
and observe their oral care routines. This, no doubt, was more than
substantial for an incentive. So we were quite confident that we
would have no problem with grabbing participants on the fly.

That evening, we made our way to this woman's house via an
old Crown Victoria station wagon taxi (with the suicide seats facing out in the back). Once we got to her town, we approached the

---

7 https://rfld.me/AveRev

8 https://youtu.be/GaHU9WLiDXU

participant's door and gave it a confident knock ... but nobody answered. We waited a few minutes longer and knocked again ... still no answer. This was before mobile phones, so we couldn't exactly call this woman on her cell. We sat and waited for 15 minutes, but then realized that our day was quickly being wasted on a participant who, for whatever reason, decided she did not want to do the study. (Perhaps she thought the $150 was too good to be true?) In a moment of desperation, Luz decided to frantically go door-to-door in this small community, hoping for a shot at someone's teeth and mouth. But to no avail.

This disastrous field trip continued. The next day we tempted fate again by preying on another unsuspecting citizen of Ciudad Tijuana. Once again, we arranged to go visit a shopkeeper's home later in the evening. Once again, we had no idea where exactly our little field visit would take us. And once again, we crammed ourselves into an old Crown Victoria station wagon. This time we were left off at what appeared to be a small village of gypsies. It was, in fact, just a typical working class abode on the outskirts of the city. I brazenly brought out my Sony DV camera with the Carl Zeiss lens and began filming the local scene as we walked through the streets to find the right home. We were very excited to find the participant's home and then to actually find her in her home!

It was a very interesting interview. The participant was a mother of two, a 9-year-old daughter and a 6-year-old son. We observed their oral care routines, which consisted of going out to the backyard to gather water from a large plastic drum (as there was no running water), after which the children vigorously brushed their teeth with your standard run-of-the-mill Colgate toothpaste and toothbrush. When we paid the mother $150 (U.S.) cash at the end of this encounter, her eyes lit up. I realized at that moment that this was probably more money than she made in a month. And so we broke another field rule: understand your surroundings and pay participants appropriately based on the context. But there was a bit of a feel-good moment here, too; the client could clearly afford the incentive money, so it was no skin off their backs.

After this first round of field visits in Tijuana, we went back about a month later for a second round, with different participants. We interviewed a relative of Luz's who lived in a canyon high above where we had visited last time. He laughed out loud when we told him that we had been down in that village only a month ago. He said with all seriousness "Don't you know that is the most dangerous area in *all* of Tijuana?" Of course, we had not known this. I thought back to the $800 Sony camera that I slung around in the streets of that village. And then I thought of my pockets full of cold, hard U.S. dollars. I laughed to myself, but thought "I need to be a little more careful in the future if I'm going to make a career of this ethnography business!"

Mary Ann Sprague: Be Prepared

I have always taken great care and a certain amount of pride in always being on time and prepared for field sites and interviews. I thank my mentors for instilling this in me early on. I always made sure that I had charged video and audio equipment, discussion guides, contact information, notebooks, extra writing implements, and power cords to carry on despite any possible problems. There has been the occasional failed battery, but I always had a spare, or my co-worker had one. It's never been a serious setback until this spring.

I was meeting my co-worker at an elementary school for a teacher interview. Teacher free time is at a premium, so I made a point of being on time and maximizing the time we had together. On this occasion, I arrived at the school parking lot a few minutes early, so I turned off my car and pulled out my iPhone to check messages. I did a mental check that I had everything in my backpack in the passenger seat. Everything was in order, so I relaxed for a couple of minutes.

Just before the meeting time, I put my phone in my pocket, got out of the car, and hit the door lock. I walked around to grab my backpack, and the door was locked. No problem, I thought, I'll go back to the driver's side and unlock it. The driver's door was locked, and the keys were still in the ignition with my equipment, questions, and paper still locked in the car!

I called my husband, and he agreed to drive home (luckily it wasn't too far) to get my spare keys and deliver them (but still a good 40-minute wait). I went into the school to meet my co-worker. She had relied on my previous level of preparation and had a notebook, but without the questions or any recording equipment.

Not wanting to reschedule, we met with the teacher. Luckily, the teacher had printed the list of questions I had emailed. I was frustrated because I didn't want to miss any part of this conversation. The teacher was a wealth of information, but the information came out at warp speed, and I worried about not being able to keep up.

Thinking about what I had with me, I realized I had my iPhone, so I recorded the entire conversation using the voice messages app and took several pictures, as did my co-worker, using our phones. I wrote my notes on the back of the question sheet from the teacher, and we had a very interesting discussion. My husband met us in the parking lot just as we left our interview. Later, I was able to retrieve the audio through iTunes and convert it to listen to it on my PC.

Everything worked out in the end, but it was a shock to my confidence. I have since begun looking at other apps to capture audio on my iPhone so that I have a better backup plan for the future, and my co-worker now carries audio equipment at least so we are always prepared.

George Ressler: Skyfall (or a View to a Kill)

Recently, I was on a project that focused on observing customer shopping behaviors at a retail space in Philadelphia. This was not the typical shop-along project because I was asked to observe customers without altering or impacting their shopping behavior. I believe that customers are aware of our presence as researchers, and it alters their shopping behavior, creating noise in the data. So, for this project, the research team really needed to become an invisible fly on the wall. To do this, we built a rig that consisted of several cameras that pushed a video feed to our research station in the back of the store. At our research station, we tracked the customer's path and tagged shopping events as they happened. In simple terms, we created a high-tech mobile solution for capturing a customer's journey that resembled something you might see James Bond using.

When the time came for the first of many fielding trips, we packed all the technology into three custom, black, hard shell cases that collectively weighed 228 pounds. We arrived at the Columbus airport extra early because we anticipated a lot of hassle from TSA for trying to fly with such "unique" equipment. At the ticket desk, our luggage was immediately flagged, and a TSA agent asked me to follow him into a back room to hand-inspect every item in the cases. As I watched from behind a yellow line of the floor, the agent tore apart my neatly packed electronics, swabbing everything for traces of explosives. All the while, he asked detailed questions about everything: "What is this? What does it do? Why do you have this?" After at least thirty minutes of explaining everything to this agent, he said that it all checked out, and I could re-pack the cases and head to the departure gate. When we arrived that afternoon in Philly, we were relieved to see our three cases thump down the baggage carousel. From the airport, we headed directly to the store to begin our setup process. Upon arriving at the store, we encountered our first real problem. Each store was supposed to have a 24-foot ladder, which would allow us to reach the ceiling to install our cameras; however, this store only had an 18-foot ladder. Being the most agile of the research team, I volunteered to climb on shelves, support beams, anything to get me up into the ceiling to install our cameras. At one point, I climbed a store shelf, holding on for dear life while clutching a 25-pound camera unit, thinking to myself that I would be so mad at myself if I died by falling off the shelf.

PHOTOS COURTESY OF LEXTANT

Once all the cameras were installed throughout the store, I began to set up the network that would pull all the video to our research station in the back room. Then problem number two arose: everything was set up perfectly, but I could not connect to the cameras from our research station. After an hour of troubleshooting, I finally realized that because our research station was behind a cement wall, the wireless signal was not reaching the cameras out in the store. In all my preparations for this trip, I had never thought to account for being behind a cement wall! The only solution was to move our router onto the store floor in front of the wall and then run an Ethernet cable to our back room research station. This meant I again climbed up to the ceiling and suspended the cable from the middle of the store to the back room. After almost an hour of monkey-climbing around the store, we had our cameras connected to the network and were ready to start collecting data.

The following two days were packed full of documenting customers' journeys. It was fascinating to observe customers shopping while slowly seeing patterns in behavior emerge. After our time in the store collecting data was over, I repeated my climb up the shelves to the ceiling to retrieve our cameras and packed up our three black cases.

We made it through TSA at the Philly airport much smoother than in Columbus and got to the gate early, leaving ample time to relax. After landing in Columbus, we waited at the baggage claim for our cases and in no time the first case clunked down the carousel. However, the other two cases never appeared. We checked their status at the baggage claim office where they informed us that our other two cases were held back for further screening because they contained "suspicious materials." We assumed they would eventually be cleared and indeed they arrived in Columbus on the next flight from Philly.

Before this all gets blamed on the TSA, those two cases did look very suspicious. I was amazed that we got them to Philly with so few problems. Each one of those cases contained a couple of huge batteries, lots of wires, and electrical boxes. Without a close inspection, the cases did look like very large, heavy bombs. So as much as I was upset at TSA for holding our cases back, I was relieved to know that they were actually catching bomb-like packages at airports and taking the time to inspect them properly.

Whenever I tell this story, I will always remember the problems we overcame with transporting and installing the technology. I can still picture myself jumping from store shelf to store shelf trying to reach the ceiling to install the cameras. But above all, I vividly remember how much I felt like James Bond when we arrived at the store with three heavy cases full of complex "spy" technology. Next time we do this kind of project, I will be bringing my tuxedo, so I could really bring the Bond persona to life.

Tamara Christensen: What the Hell? Don't You Knock?

My first trip to New Jersey for fieldwork involved two memorable events: a blizzard and a bathroom blitz.

Two days before we departed for New Jersey, I received an email request from my client to rent the biggest SUV available. A huge snowstorm was pounding the Northeast, and he wanted to feel safe as we ventured into the streets and highways of various townships for a week of in-home interviews. I obliged and was glad I did. The evening we arrived, we found the streets covered with snow, and the plows were evidently having trouble keeping up.

I kept getting rescheduling calls from the recruiter. Participants were cancelling because of the weather. This seemed strange, given the fact that *we* were the ones traveling to their homes, and they didn't have to go anywhere! It felt like a game of musical chairs as we continually shifted and rescheduled. It was impossible to predict if we would be able to complete the targeted number of interviews during our week-long visit. In fact, it was even difficult to predict if we would be able to leave town at the end of the week because the airport was canceling flights every day.

There were three of us in the field: myself, a videographer, and the client. We all met for breakfast the first morning while the car warmed up. It took 30 minutes to melt the layers of ice that had accumulated overnight on the windshield. Fortunately, the heater had kicked in by the time we all piled into the SUV and headed out for our first interview of the week, giving ourselves ample time to arrive at our destination.

Instead of the 30 minutes suggested by Google Maps, we arrived an hour later at our destination, a narrow residential street of two-story, beige brick duplexes still decorated for the Christmas holiday. Plows had left six-foot tall snowbanks on either side of the street, and cars were parked in tight spaces carved out by the residents. Sadly, it appeared that most of those residents didn't have an SUV as big as our rental. We circled the area for fifteen minutes before we found a gap large enough to park in.

We were there to interview a young woman in her 20s, a nurse. She welcomed us into the living room where we set up our cameras and found places to sit among her teddy bear collection and her floor-to-ceiling cabinet, which contained an homage to Michael Jackson. Her mother appeared in a short fuzzy black robe. "I've been doing focus groups for years. No one ever asked to come to this house before. Why do you want to go to people's houses?" We explained the nature of our visit and commenced with the interview.

For the first half hour of the interview, the mother came in and out of the room, answering and asking questions and reiterating her concerns about our presence and intentions. Each time, the daughter would suspend her responses to address the interruption, urging her mother out of the room. "We always meet at Dunkin' Donuts. That's the place to go ... MA! They're here to talk to me. Let me do this!" "I always stop on my way to work to pick up an iced tea ... MA! Go get dressed already!" "I love those little facts on the lid. They are so cute ... MA! Enough! Quit interrupting us!" No matter what the daughter said, the mother would return every few minutes to listen and contribute.

I realized shortly into the interview that, in our flurry of inclement travel, I had neglected to honor one of the cardinal rules of interviewing: "Go before you arrive." I ignored my biological needs as long as I could, but the morning's coffee didn't help. I finally had to excuse myself for a restroom break.

"It's just there in the hall, on the right," said the nurse, pointing down the mirrored hallway.

I excused myself and walked to the bathroom door. It was open a few inches, so I pushed it. There in the bright pink-and-black tiled bathroom stood the mother, facing the toilet with her little black robe hiked up above the waist, her backside completely exposed.

She turned before I could retreat. "What the Hell? Don't you knock?" I felt blood rush warmly to my face.

"I'm so sorry," I said, backing out and closing the door behind (or rather, in front of) me. "I'm so sorry," I continued, "the door was open. I didn't realize anyone was in there. I'm so sorry."

I swiftly returned to the living room.

"I'm so sorry," I told the nurse. "The door was open a crack, so I just went in, and I walked in on your mother. I am sure I've upset her."

"Ha! Don't worry. She'll be fine," she consoled me. "Maybe she'll leave us alone now."

I wasn't sure I would be fine. I tried to concentrate on the interview, the purpose of our visit, the friendly nurse who gave us a detailed tour of the kitchen drawers. But images of her mother's bare behind kept flashing in my mind. She was right, sort of, about her mother leaving us alone. For the remaining hour, we didn't hear a word from the woman, although she kept appearing (now fully clothed) wherever we were. She said nothing. She just looked at me with a glare that felt as icy as the windshield that awaited us outside.

Our first stop was a Dunkin' Donuts where I was finally able to relieve myself.

Jenn Downs: Burns, Bandages, and BBQ

I was out of town with a colleague for a full-day customer visit, and while getting ready for the day, I burned my thumb pretty badly on my hair straightening iron. It was the kind of burn you can soothe for about two seconds before it makes you roll your eyes back and cry out in pain. We'd planned ahead and given ourselves plenty of time to get ready that morning, so we had a few extra minutes to find some burn cream. I ran down to the front desk of our hotel to see if they had a first aid kit. They did not. However, one of the hotel staff offered me a packet of mustard to soothe the burn, some kind of Southern old wives' tale. I don't usually believe in old Southern food-on-skin remedies, but I wanted it to work. So I slathered the burn in mustard, hoping for the best. This remedy was not the best.

Two seconds later, I was again whimpering in pain. I filled a cup with ice water and stuck my thumb in the cup. This provided a tremendous amount of relief, while being completely impractical. So we sped out to find a drugstore.

Being on the outskirts of a college town, there weren't many places to find first aid items, but we did find a grocery store open before 8 a.m. I bought everything—burn cream, aloe, bandages, anything that looked like it might work, just in case. But nothing I purchased worked! Nothing but the cup of ice water could stop me from visibly wincing. We were running out of time and had to head to our meeting, hoping for some kind of miracle.

My colleague and I found our way to our customer's office and had to wait for our interviewees to come get us from another part of the building. Fortunately, the front desk person at the office was keenly observant. Before I could even say a word, she'd found a refill of ice water for my aching thumb. And then it was time. We went in to meet our customers, my thumb fully immersed in this cup of water.

I should mention that we worked for a really creative and weird company, and we were visiting a very conservative and traditional Southern company. We were feeling more than a little out of our element. I thought for a moment that the interview was going to be a disaster, but my thumb on ice was actually a nice icebreaker (pun not intended).

Then I spilled the cup of ice water all over their conference room table.

In that moment, all I could do was laugh at myself and let everyone laugh with me. We continued the interview as I was cleaning up the mess—calmly and confidently.

In the end, it turned out to be a great interview and gave the guys at the company something to joke with us about over a BBQ lunch. Imagine trying to eat ribs with one thumb wrapped in gauze and burn cream. My confidence through all the awkwardness ended up making them feel comfortable with having strangers in their office all day, and we got great information we probably wouldn't have otherwise. Sometimes, you just have to roll with it.

Takeaways

- **Write down the key things you need to remember.** Writing down "turn on the video camera" or "give the incentive to the participant" are tiny things you can do in the present to make life just a bit simpler for your future self. Once it's written down (on a planning worksheet or an interview guide), then you are relieved of having to keep it in mind.

- **Be prepared for things to go wrong.** Acknowledging that possibility ahead of time means that you won't be as surprised if or when something does happen, and it puts you in a better state to respond.

- **Know that when one thing goes wrong, it's highly likely that other things will go wrong.** Once you've had one thing fail, remind yourself that you are more vulnerable to another thing going wrong. Even if you can't prevent it, you can prepare emotionally.

- **Manage your gear (even if it's as basic as a notepad and an audio recorder) and know that it requires attention to detail.** In this basic example, you should check that you have sufficient blank pages, that you have more than one pen, that the pens have ink, that there's enough free storage space on your recording device, and that you have battery power to get through the interview. Throw in a video camera with a tripod, battery packs, and chargers, and there's just that much more to pay attention to.

- **Anticipate how you will handle your data.** While you can hold onto physical artifacts like notes, digital data can be a problem, especially if you're on the road. Video files are huge (even with the camera set to a lower quality). Some audio recorders also produce huge files. Make sure that you have space on another device (such as a laptop or a portable hard drive). Don't expect to be able to upload large files, especially if you are using hotel Wi-Fi.

- **Give some thought to backup plans and work-arounds.** If your audio recorder breaks, can you record on your mobile phone? If your interview guide gets rained on, can you remember enough questions to lead the interview? You can't prepare an alternative to everything, but some anticipatory thinking will help you problem-solve in the moment.

- **You have to take care of yourself.** Get enough sleep, get something to eat, and find a bathroom. Make a detailed plan with your team about where and when you will take care of those needs.

Those Exasperating Participants

Photo by Steve Portigal

It feels awfully tone-deaf for me to be writing about participants in any sort of negative way. Researchers cherish participants. We advocate for them. We deride others who judge, or even worse, express contempt for participants. Heck, we *love* our participants!

In a blog post,[1] Antonella Pavese compares her connection with research participants to the feeling of being in love: "Do you remember that time you fell madly in love with somebody? Or when your child was born? The other became the object of unlimited interest and fascination. You perceived everything the loved one did or said as something special and unique. When you are in love, you want to know everything about the other person, almost to absorb his or her essence. For just a moment, you are more interested in them than in yourself." We listen intently to our participants and form a strong connection with them. We take that connection with us, and as we advocate for them with our colleagues and clients, we act on that feeling of love.

But using the word *participant* masks the fact that we're dealing with *people*. Any endeavor that involves people will have glitches. Our whole enterprise depends on us getting to people who are willing to talk with us, share with us, allow us to observe them, play with our clever apparatus, and so on. So it's to be expected that sometimes those things don't work out.

Sometimes the people we're doing research with can't help us. Sometimes they won't. Sometimes they aren't even around to help. Sometimes they are just out to work the system for their own benefit, and sometimes they are perplexingly, elusively challenging.

I interviewed a man in a large home in a gated community who presumably didn't "need" the honorarium but was incredibly hostile the entire time, which was unpleasant but also confounding because I couldn't understand why he agreed to do something he so obviously did not want to do. I interviewed another man in an apartment building where the lobby smelled of urine, and he didn't own the

---

1 http://rfld.me/RsrcLuv

credit card he told me he owned, and explained his aspirations were to "get myself a 'rich bitch.'" I interviewed an exceptionally friendly person who was filled with detailed stories, but had absolutely zero insight about himself and was unable to reflect or even explain anything; the interview never went beyond his reporting of facts. And I was let into a woman's apartment to interview her, while she finished her phone call scheduling her next interview. After hearing about some other apartment in another city where her children lived, we asked to see some computer activity, and she opened up a folder named *Portigal* to show "examples." As far as we could tell, none of what she told us was true, and she was a known "frequent flyer" in the San Francisco Bay Area user research scene. I interviewed a very forthcoming Silicon Valley executive in his home, as he described his side business in a way that utterly, distressingly contradicted what he had told the recruiter.

NOTE IT'S HARD TO BELIEVE IN DISHONESTY

When it starts to dawn on me that my participant is critically different from what I was expecting, it's uncomfortable. I feel chagrin for having screwed up (a lazy recruiter or a poor screener) and letting this person get into the study. It must be my fault! It's devastating to think that I'm face-to-face with someone, listening intently and building rapport, and yet they lied to the recruiter and are lying to me now. The practice of research is predicated on a presumption of honesty, and what do I do with someone who thinks nothing of boldly lying? It's easier to blame myself— and the recruiting process—rather than confronting that idea (to say nothing of confronting the participant).

In this chapter, Gerry Gaffney finds himself with the wrong type of participant but examines what he learns anyway. Leo Frishberg and Doug Cooke describe their experiences in traveling around the world to see participants who are unavailable, literally. Daria Loi and Patricia Colley share their stories about trying to do research with people who just weren't fully available to them, and Cordy Swope meets his own frequent flyer.

There's plenty of pushback about the ineffectiveness of focus groups. But what is most disturbing to me is how sitting behind the glass window curtails our empathy. It's as if the design of the environment encourages us to sit in judgment while munching on overpriced M&Ms.

I once ran a dynamic session in one of those rooms and then came back to the observation room at the end of the evening to chat with the team. There I met my client's new Director of Research, who, in summing up what she had heard, referred to one of the participants as "That one over there (pointing at where she had been sitting), you know, Blondie." (The woman in question was blonde, but her name was definitely not Blondie.) I was shocked that a researcher would speak this way, especially to her new colleagues. I never learned if that was typical for her or a nervous reaction.

A year later, working with another organization, I was behind the two-way mirror myself and began to feel the itch of judgments accruing. Having had the earlier unhappy experience of observing a researcher dismiss focus group participants, I was able to recognize my own feelings and focus on trying to feel connected with the people in the room. Still, I much prefer to do research in a manner that fosters feelings of empathy rather than a methodology that requires making an effort to overcome apathy and disdain.

Gerry Gaffney: Right to Be Wrong

I was researching, with my colleague Patrizia Bordignon, how people thought about and dealt with home renovations.

One of the methods was a diary study ("cultural probe"), and we had carefully recruited—or so we believed—a small set of participants with whom we would work for several weeks.

Warning bells sounded fairly early with one of the participants, who showed up very late for the initial briefing. These things can happen, so we ran a separate briefing session for him, gave him his kit of reporting materials (camera, diary and so on), and sent him on his way. Let's call him Mr. W.

Three days after the briefing, we telephoned each of the participants. It's a good idea to do this to remind people about their commitment, to redirect as necessary, and to address any issues that arise. All our participants were on track, with the notable exception of Mr. W, who seemed somewhat evasive in his answers.

At the end of the first week, we visited the participants. Again, this is good practice; it's an opportunity to see how the data is being gathered, and what changes might be needed to the process. We also use that opportunity to make a partial payment to the participants, which can serve as a nice motivation.

We were delighted with what we saw. Participants had kept bills and receipts, photographs, and magazine clippings; they showed us their renovations or their plans; and we were confident that we were getting plenty of highly relevant data.

When we visited Mr. W's house, however, it was evident from the first moment that his home was different. The front gate didn't work properly, and the hinges squeaked; the garden was unkempt, and the house had an overall sense of dilapidation. Inside it was a similar story. Every room was in dire need of immediate restorative work, but none was evident. I felt a tad depressed as we drank tea from cracked mugs and listened to Mr. W list the things that needed to be fixed.

PHOTO BY GERRY GAFFNEY

Mr. W was not an enthusiastic renovator. His house represented a series of urgent and necessary tasks, none of which had been tackled.

It looked like we would collect no useful data from Mr. W, and as we traveled back to the office, we talked about our disappointment and reexamined our recruiting strategy.

However, as we moved into data analysis, we found ourselves referring quite often to Mr. W, and gradually came to realize (no doubt this should have been obvious earlier) that Mr. W's world was, in fact, directly relevant to our project. While the enthusiastic renovator was undoubtedly a key consideration, the unenthused or reluctant could also present great opportunities. Their needs and goals were different, their attitudes were different, and the way that we would design for those characteristics was different.

In many ways, Mr. W was an ideal participant specifically because he didn't fit our expectations. He challenged the underpinnings of the project, and he forced us to examine our design decisions in a much more rigorous fashion.

I often reflect back on this experience when I'm doing user research, and I specifically watch out for negative reactions and experiences, because they can often teach us things that we might not otherwise learn.

I still believe it's important to recruit carefully, but perhaps we should be more open to the idea that the "wrong" participant is sometimes precisely the right one.

Leo Frishberg: No, We Really Meant the User

Our team was embarking on an ambitious, multi-country contextual inquiry effort. We had created our sample cells, identified the right industries, established a great relationship with our sales team, and done *All the Right Things Up Front* to make the effort a success.

Working from Oregon with prospective participants in Bangalore is never an easy prospect; introducing a new research technique at the same time raised the stakes.

Several weeks in advance of the interviews, we had contacted our sales team in-country explaining the process: we needed individuals who were currently working with our equipment and willing to let us observe them working in their labs, in situ.

Everyone claimed to understand. We arrived in-country, and I confirmed the arrangements, on the telephone, with the sales team. "Yes," they confirmed, "we've found exactly who you are looking for."

We arrived at our first interview in a gorgeous sparkling new office building and were led to an upstairs glass-enclosed conference room. Presently, a manager-type entered, clearly expecting to hold court with us.

I began the discussion with a recap of our expectations and a quick sanity check with the individual.

"So," I began, "We are looking forward to working with an actual user in the lab. Are you going to work with us today?"

"No," he said, dismissively. "I'm the team manager. I can tell you everything that's wrong with your equipment. I've polled the team and have collected answers from all of them."

It's at times like this, having flown 10,000 miles, having spent as much time as I had setting things up, that I lose a part of my conscious brain. I could feel the anger rising, but I knew that wouldn't help improve the situation.

Instead, I signaled to the sales guy sitting next to me that as far as I was concerned, the interview was over, and we could pack up to go to our next meeting. Here's where the details get sketchy, but I know he said something in English to the manager, and whatever magic words he uttered, the manager smiled and nodded, suggesting he could definitely get the lead engineer to help us. He left to find the guy.

A few minutes later, the engineer entered the room, curious as to what the group was doing there. We began the front part of the interview, and it was clear he was the right guy. After explaining what we were planning to do, we asked if he had any questions or needed any further explanation.

'No," he said. "You want to see me work with the equipment. I don't have anything to do today, but I could show you what I was doing last week."

That was fine, we agreed.

"OK. Just give me a few minutes, and I'll bring you back. ... "

Imagining what he might be doing in those few minutes, I stopped him. "Uhhh, what would you be doing between now and then?"

"Oh," he assured us. "I'm just going to get the equipment all set up."

"Great!" We practically shouted. "That would be great! We'd be happy to watch you do that!"

He smiled, as if hoping we had taken our medication. "I'm not sure what you'll find so interesting about my pulling the machines off the shelf, but come on along." And with that, he led us to his lab.

Doug Cooke: Knock-Knock! Who's There?

In a recent research and strategy project focused on defining a new global platform for a medical device, our research plan required us to shadow clinicians and others as they used existing devices in the "context of care." With issues like HIPAA[2] protecting patient privacy and other security issues at big urban hospitals in the U.S., our team decided that conducting research in Europe provided a better opportunity to understand these devices and their users.

Planning started with all the usual steps: multi-day client sessions to assess the domain, issues, and problems; auditing reams of client data and documents; becoming familiar with competitive products, etc. We developed a research protocol that went through many rounds of revision with a large, multi-location client team arriving at a clear understanding of relevant and important user issues. We developed screening criteria for participating medical institutions. Pilot studies were run at United States hospitals. Months of preparation were spent in making sure our research team was fully prepared to bring back insights and perspectives that would help define the next generation global respirator platform. Ready, set, on to Europe!

Our first stop was at a hospital in Wales. They had lined up the appropriate people for us to shadow and interview, including department heads, physicians, and medical techs. We spent two days shadowing, probing, and gathering, and everything worked according to plan. Wahoo!

At our second stop in London (hauling two large model cases that would not fit into London's very spacious cabs), we arrived at the check-in desk and asked to see Dr. Smith (or so we'll call him). Upon arrival at his department wing, we learned that Dr. Smith was not in. Even more concerning was that Dr. Smith was out of the country at a conference and had not let anyone else know we were coming. After speaking with a few more people, the answer was "Please come back

---

2 The Health Insurance Portability and Accountability Act:
   http://www.hhs.gov/hipaa

at another time when the doctor is in." Ouch! In spite of all the planning, effort, and resources to get here, a few uncooperative people were about to jeopardize our research program.

How could this happen? Well, I ignored one of my primary rules: never let the client take on a critical path item that could endanger the project's success and my firm's reputation. Specifically, because of the difficulty of gaining access to the right people and institutions, and extremely high costs if we were to use a traditional recruiting process, our client took on the responsibility of arranging our visits to hospitals throughout Europe. Few clients understand the level of effort needed to screen, schedule, and triple-confirm each participant. When the "research gig" is complex and requires the participation of a number of people carefully choreographed in a short time, it is essential to have a dedicated, experienced resource to make that happen.

We made it all work in the end. With no Dr. Smith and an apparent dead-end, we literally started on-the-spot networking, walking up and introducing ourselves to doctor after doctor until we had made some friends who would grant us two days of access in the ICU and ER. It worked out in the end, but presented unforeseen delays and stress to an already pressure-filled project. Painful, but constructive outcomes, nonetheless.

The rest of the trip in Germany and Italy presented various levels of preparedness on the part of the hospitals we visited. Some hospitals were planning on hosting us for our full two-day itinerary, and some were expecting only a few hours' meeting (which we were able to extend by turning on our best charm).

I have always been a very careful planner and can fastidiously orchestrate research logistics. I know what it takes to gather user insights. But the lessons learned from this European research foray are a clear reminder that whenever I can, I must control the recruiting and scheduling process. I hope to never again knock on any unsuspecting doors.

Daria Loi: Researcher Thresholds

Several years ago, a colleague and I traveled to Sweden, Indonesia, and China for a study of storage practices in homes. We were particularly interested in observing everyday activities related to the "stuff" one owns, like clustering, archiving, organizing, disposing, sharing, holding, recycling, and so on. The goal was to gather useful insights from the analog world to better understand how people might deal with data in the digital one.

In each city, we recruited a number of participants to be interviewed twice and to complete a cultural probe during the week between the interviews. The first interview (about three hours) started by focusing on baseline data for the first 60–90 minutes, and then shifted to a home tour in which we would go room by room, observing the environment and asking questions arising from what we noticed or from what the participant indicated during the baseline interview. During this part of the first interview, we would often find ourselves opening drawers, cupboards, wardrobes, and the like, with participants' permission, of course.

There is nothing more fascinating than seeing what people do with their stuff. To some extent, you see yourself and your own behaviors in action, and in other cases, you have to be prepared to find the most obscure things in those drawers—so obscure that even their owners are perplexed when they rediscover them!

I have fond memories of a young and bright Swedish woman laughing with puzzled surprise when she discovered the enormous amount of candles she managed to accumulate and that all those candles were in the same drawer as a flyswatter she did not recall owning. I still giggle when I think of a beautiful Indonesian family taking us in their storage room, to discover they had six to seven identical broken appliances. I still remember the puzzlement of the husband, trying to work out how on earth that accumulation happened. And again, I always smile with affection and admiration when I think of a Chinese painter and his lovely wife showing us their feng-shui based order of things.

During this quite long study (a bit more than two weeks in the field for each country, long for corporate research), one of our many adventures was about a Chengdu-based participant, often code-named "the interviewee from hell."

It all started in the morning at 9 a.m.—the first interview for that day. We rang the bell of an apartment, but no response. After a few minutes, we tried again, but still nothing. We started feeling edgy, as we did not want to be culturally inappropriate or pushy. Yet suddenly the door opened to reveal a young pajama-clad woman with puffy eyes who was evidently just out of bed.

The young lady, who here will remain unnamed, looked at us evidently annoyed, flashing "how dare you wake me up" eyes, and asked us what we wanted. The translator explained that we were there for the interview, and she told us she was pretty sure we were one day early.

My colleague and I began thinking of ways to accommodate her interview another day, but the participant let us in—even though we feared this was not the best premise for the best interview.

After the usual preambles and consent form sign-offs, we set up our video gear and proceeded with the first part of the interview. I should have immediately realized something was off when I saw the participant clutching her mobile phone with great intimacy—the glued-on-my-body type of intimacy. But no, her behavior did not immediately ring the "this is going to be a disaster" bell, and we started with the interview, with me taking charge of picture/video taking activities.

There is something rather cool about framing another human being through a camera. You observe little details even more deeply. And now, all the little details immediately rang the infamous "this *is* going to be a disaster interview" bell. For the rest of the interview, the following scenario occurred over and over again:

- Colleague asked a question while participant checked her phone (text, emails, Internet).

- Participant responded with "yes," "no," and "hmm ... I think so" type of answers.

- Our facial expressions were incredulous.

- Participant continued checking her phone, rarely looking up or even acknowledging someone was asking her questions.

This loop goes on and on. After a while, we tried to send a *subliminal* message by asking whether she would prefer to meet another time since she seemed busy (read: distracted and totally unengaged). The young lady looked at us (finally!) and said, "No, it's fine. Let's do it now." (Read: this is tedious already; you interrupted my beauty sleep, so let's get it over and done with it.)

So ... we went on. After a while, I started having the giggles, intrigued by the evidently dysfunctional situation. I felt tempted to suggest we refocus the interview on her mobile phone usage (evidently her passion), to learn something useful instead of pushing a cart into such a void-of-usefulness corner. But I didn't suggest it. Instead, I kept going. Maybe I was in shock. Maybe I was so entertained by her behaviors that I wanted to see how far she could go. Maybe both. Hard to tell—these things happen fast, and it is often easier to think about the right thing to do retrospectively.

Anyway, the rest of the interview continued along the same lines, with the exception of the home tour part, where my pictures were not of a user handling her phone while on a couch, but those of shoulders hunched over a phone. During the tour, the verbal part of the interview shifted from yes/no answers to a number of grunts and monosyllables.

After three hours, we finally left. We looked at each other in total puzzlement, unsure if we should cry, laugh, or have a meltdown. We would have been totally entitled to have one. Instead, we kept our cool and moved on (aside from a few colorful words that I won't put in writing). It was a testing-your-patience-thresholds kind of day.

But the fun part was not over yet, because after a week, we had a second interview scheduled!

This second interview was definitely much more colorful. Instead of taking pictures of a participant and her phone, I managed to take pictures of serious multitasking in action: for instance, send texts and check your social network on the phone with the left hand while checking the stock exchange on the laptop with the right hand. And do not forget the yes/no/grunt answers and minimal level of auditory attention paid to us.

If you were to ask me what I learned from this participant, I would say *lots*.

If you instead asked: Did you learn anything useful for your project? *Not a thing* would be my answer.

Regardless, this experience led to a good story to share and helped me have a different appreciation for researchers' thresholds.

Patricia Colley: The Hidden Persuader

In 1984, I was 23 and working for a market and social research firm in San Antonio, Texas. They sent me down to McAllen to collect voter opinions on the upcoming national elections. McAllen is a sleepy little town near the bottom tip of the state, just a few miles from the Mexican border, mainly populated with low-to-moderate income Hispanic families.

I was on my second day of door-to-door polling, asking voters their opinions on policy matters and their thoughts on the state and presidential candidates. I was getting a high rate of interview completions, with lots of useful data. After four years in market and social research, I was quite confident in my neutral, non-threatening "aw shucks, I'm just one of you" act, and its ability to deliver great results.

But my confidence was shaken when I met Maria, a shy housewife in her early 30s.

It was about 4 p.m. on a warm, dry Thursday afternoon when I knocked on the door of a modest, well-kept ranch house in a suburban section of McAllen. Maria opened the door partway. She was half-hiding behind it, sizing me up like a rabbit peering through tall grass at a coyote in the distance ... curious, but poised to flee.

I explained that I was gathering public opinions on the upcoming elections, and after she agreed, we began the interview.

Me: "Now, thinking about (Candidate X), what comes to mind?"

Maria: "Uhh, I don't know? Is he a good guy?"

Me (shrinking): "Well, I really don't have any thoughts on (Candidate X). Besides, my bosses didn't send me all this way to talk about my opinions. He wants to know your opinion."

Maria: "I don't know. He seems OK?"

Now, I didn't think Maria was incapable of forming opinions. I suspect she had simply never been asked to share her thoughts about such important things. And she might never be asked again. But on this day, I was determined to make her opinion count.

Me: "Well, you've heard of him, maybe seen him on TV?"

Maria: "Yes."

Me: "So, what did you think of him? Is he someone you would vote for?"

Maria: "Um ... (pause)"

Her eyes darted across my face, scanning every crease and twitch, searching for clues. Those big rabbit eyes begged mutely for help. I stared back, apologetically. I took a few slow breaths, trying to ground us both, so she might relax into talking more naturally. Each time she hesitated, I carefully repeated the question, altering the wording and inflection to make it sound as simple and benign as possible.

Me: "Really, we're just interested in what you think. Whatever you think is fine. Do you think you'll vote for him, or not?"

Maria: "Uh ... yes?" (seeing no reaction from me) "No?"

Me: "OK, that's fine. Alright. Now, thinking about (Issue A), is that important to you? Do you think it's good or bad?"

Maria: "Uhh ... I think it's good?"

The back and forth went on for several minutes. I tried to be neutral and free of any emotional expression, but my contortions only intensified the awkwardness. I was failing miserably to collect any genuine responses from Maria. A hot wave of panic washed over me. How can I get this back on track?

I quit fighting it, and fell back on connecting with Maria as a person. I began riffing on her responses, affirming and adding detail to them. While trying not to reveal my personal opinions, I offered supportive words and gestures to elevate everything she said, so that she might open up and elaborate. Eventually, her answers flowed a bit more freely.

Me: "So, what about the presidential candidates?"

Maria: "I guess I'll vote for (presidential candidate B)."

Me: "Great! Is it because he is for (issue B)?"

Maria: "Oh, that's good. Yeah, (B) is good for us."

I felt I was way off book. It seemed impossible not to sway her answers. Well, at least she was talking. Finally, we got to the end. Walking back to my car, I breathed a huge sigh of relief. The hardest interview I'd ever done was over. I went out for a well-earned drink and a tragicomic debriefing with my co-workers.

Sometimes you just get a dud subject, but something about that 15-minute exchange with Maria struck a deeper chord in me. As I drove out of town, troubling questions lingered. What is the value of a skewed interview? Was this the only time I'd failed to be impartial? Or had this been happening all along, in more subtle ways? How can I ever know that the data I'm collecting is pure?

Maria taught me two important things that day.

- People make stuff up as they go along. And we can't always see the flaws in self-reporting.

- The observer effect is unavoidable. Interviewers shade their work in unpredictable ways.

I'm as diligent as ever about delivering valuable insight through my research. But ever since that incident in McAllen, I draw my conclusions with a fuzzy border, in humble deference to flawed inputs and shadow projections, on both sides of the clipboard.

Cordy Swope: A Crisis of Credibility

IDEO. NYC. Early 2010.

I had been summoned from Europe to lead a project about the future of education in the U.S. At IDEO, there is a well-established code of ethics for site visits. This code takes extra measures to protect the privacy of informants, especially their identities and contact data. IDEO also has sensible, street-smart guidelines for fieldwork in sketchy environments. In previous jobs, I had seen a situation in which two of my female design researchers had to go to remote, sparsely populated parts of the Midwest and visit big, burly, smiling men who stored every conceivable power tool in their dungeon-like tornado cellars.

There is never a shortage of people in NYC, though, and recruiting there offers many delights. For instance, NYC is one of only several places where it is possible to recruit for impossibly specific profiles like: "Seeking 3 single dads who have volunteered with their children at a local charity organization within the past 2 weeks, and who also must struggle with their own gender identity, and make at least $150K/year." In the Tristate, if you are one in a million, by definition there are at least 22 of you.

Our recruiter used Craigslist for most projects and straightaway found us one of our targets: a working mother who had successfully completed a BA online while still raising a family. I had a new team, and my associate design researcher was an eager, empathic and articulate ethnographer doing her first project at IDEO. We headed out to Inwood in Brooklyn for our first site visit, hoping to get insights from this working, baccalaureate mom.

During the ride, I played the senior mentor guy, offering advice about doing ethnography "in a design context." We arrived at the address in Inwood, an obscure part of Brooklyn that looks like a sad, dilapidated part of Queens that, in turn, tries to look like a nondescript suburb in Long Island. We were buzzed into the building, walked up to a door, and were greeted by a large woman with a curly red mane of hair. Her name was "Roberta-but-call-me-Bert."

She let us in. The apartment was dim. It smelled of litter box mixed with burnt Dinty Moore beef stew that Ramon, Roberta-call-me-Bert's husband had overheated on the stove. The dingy plaster walls were covered in old shopping lists, written in a mangled scrawl, that suggested vaguely menacing pathologies and personality disorders suffered by their author.

The sofa we sat on smelled of cat piss, and the living room offered up no pretense of ever having been cleaned. We sat up straight, made eye contact in that standard, pious, non-judgmental manner that earnest ethnographers often adopt. We began the paperwork. We were offered water and politely declined.

I asked her about work, family, free time—all of the perfunctory questions before we got into her BA experience. Since I was the seasoned professional, I led the discussion, "Tell me a story about your favorite class." "Did you make friends with your classmates?" "Do you still keep in touch?" Since my associate was taking notes, I focused on keeping the discussion moving and letting Roberta-call-me-Bert lead us to all sorts of exciting insights.

The trouble was, she didn't.

"Oh, I don't remember much about that class," she said about her favorite statistics course she took just before graduating 18 months ago. "Yeah, I pretty much kept to myself, because I had to work and raise a family, you know?" I nodded my head earnestly.

I began asking her questions about change. "Do you view your daughter's education differently now since you got the degree?" "Not really," she said, as her daughter ate ice cream from a container while watching a YouTube video about dog fighting.

We eventually went on our way. Once out the door, I was about to launch into the debrief. Since I was the experienced one, I was going to teach my associate a simple, time-honored 20-minute structure I often use for debriefs: Interesting Behaviors/Motivations and Drivers/Problems and Frustrations/Opportunities.

I noticed that she was grimacing.

"What's wrong?" I asked.

"That was a waste," she replied.

"What do you mean?" I asked.

"She lied, she never went to college."

I was gobsmacked.

And she was absolutely right.

There were no interesting behaviors. There were no drivers or motivations. There were no problems or frustrations. There were no opportunities.

There was no diploma. It was "packed away somewhere."

Takeaways

- **It goes without saying (but let's say it anyway) that good recruiting is essential.** Where you can, screen for softer qualities like articulateness and engagement. It's the researcher's job to probe and follow up, ask good questions, and help draw out the participant, but there's some baseline of social interactivity below which doing this type of interview may be a lost cause. During the screening process, ask them to tell a story as a way to gauge how easily—and how well—they express themselves. You may work with a recruiter to arrange interviews, but your first step after the interviews are scheduled can be an introductory call during which you can assess a participant's suitability. With geographic and cultural distance, this becomes less trivial, but it's worth working out.

- **The more you invest in doing the fieldwork (e.g., travel) the more you should consider backup plans.** It's one thing to drive across town for a no-show participant; it's quite another to fly to another continent. Even discussing with the rest of the team how you might handle the unexpected can prepare you to improvise. Invest in recruiting additional participants (who receive a reduced incentive if they aren't interviewed) in case scheduled participants cancel or aren't suitable.

- **Accept that failures will happen.** A key element of interviewing people in the field is that you can't always see at the time what is being revealed from the experience. So those failures may—sometimes, at least—turn out to be inspiring or informative in other ways than what you had expected.

We returned to the office. Another colleague was leading a project in men's fashion and desperately trying to recruit shop-along dyads of couples in their 40s and 50s where wives selected the husband's clothes. She said they had already recruited one couple on Craigslist and that her name was Roberta from Inwood, Brooklyn.

- **If you find yourself challenged to engage your participant in the interview you had hoped to conduct, look for a way to change the conversation to something that is more engaging to the participant.** This may provide a conversational bridge to the topics you were planning on discussing. Or it may reveal analogous perspectives or attitudes that you can apply to your own topics.

- **If an interview is going badly, you should stick with it anyway.** You've made the investment in time to get that interview. You've already done the work to recruit this participant, and you still have to pay them an incentive. By the time things are feeling hopeless, you might be able to get back an hour of your time. But what a great opportunity to get creative with your interview techniques! You have nothing to lose. Maybe you'll get somewhere, maybe you won't.

- **Don't assign blame when you meet a dishonest participant.** It's hard enough to try and learn from a participant. When you start to feel that something is wrong with the situation, try not to add the additional distraction of worrying about how this happened. If you're a basically honest person (and this would be a weird type of work to be doing if you weren't), then trying to have an authentic interaction with a calmly dishonest person is unsettling. Blaming yourself or others (and the attendant frustration or disappointment) is a way to avoid confronting that possibility. But you can't ascertain during the interview whether there's been an oversight in the process, a mix-up, or outright deception. So leave the resolution until later and carry on. Again, you have nothing to lose.

YOU CAN SEE
THE SUN!
For Free

CHAPTER 3

Control Is
an Illusion

Photo by Steve Portigal

You know about this room. It's a really big room. It's something more than a room, but that's the best word we know to describe this space, this enclosure of technology and urgency. You know about this room—it's clean and organized and is populated by an abundance of uniformed workers in headsets, seated at workstations before a massive wall-sized video display. Meanwhile, an intense man in eyeglasses and shirt sleeves is shouting instructions. Whatever optimism we might have felt at one point has now devolved into grim concern.

This is the Control Room. Any movie that shows us a Control Room is tipping its hand broadly: things are soon going to be very badly *Out Of Control*. This highly designed system is hubris made manifest, and we're all gonna see what happens when its dwellers encounter unanticipated circumstances. The intel is wrong! The monster is impervious to our weapons! The enemy agent has spotted the surveillance team! The target is still in the safe house! The Control Room is a monument to the planning, systems, routines, processes, and procedures that lead to success, but its brittleness is revealed when what's required is improvisation.

The Control Room (and its inhabitants) is safely ensconced in a bunker, a safe house, at headquarters. But the real action—which they watch semi-helplessly on that wall-sized video display—is out in the field. If there is to be any success today, it will be because of a field team that rejects the naïveté of the Control Room.

This gulf between abstracted plans and on-the-ground reality is a real concern to the researcher. The realities we'll read about here aren't as epic and the body count is far lower than in film, but the stories remind us that you can't anticipate all of what will happen in the field. We anticipate our destinations in their optimal versions, but unanticipated ordinary and extraordinary occurrences are coming for us.

Ironically, the bonus value of this kind of research is in the things that you can't anticipate—that you'd never think to ask about—but discover once you enter the context you're interested in. If you go to a customer's site, you can't control what's going on in their business that day, whether it's the management, as Diane Loviglio discovers, or the technology, as Vanessa Pfafflin experiences. If you do research in public, you can't plan for who else will be there or what will take place. Elaine Ann and Ryan DeGorter remind us that if you are working with people, you can't control what else might happen with them on any given day. Nicolas Nova and Elaine Fukuda run into some interesting people during their fieldwork. The Control Room manifests a belief that you can anticipate and design for anything, but the lesson we take from the drama is that we will fail if we believe that.

Diane Loviglio: Interrupted Interview

We walked down a nondescript hallway, me and my team's designer and engineer. It was the first time the three of us had been in the field together. I was confident and excited, but also a little nervous that our engineer would start asking off-topic questions like "How many lines of code did that take?" during the interview. We found the door of the gaming studio, and we walked inside—straight into the kitchen. The walls were brightly painted, the plan was open, the kitchen was right in front of us, but there was no reception area in sight. So now the three of us were just standing in the hustle and bustle of the studio and weren't sure where to go next. We felt a little awkward. Eventually, I started to text our host, but she appeared before I finished typing the message.

Melissa (that's what I'll call her) warmly greeted us. She had high energy, but you could also tell things were a little chaotic that day. She walked us 500 feet to one of their two conference rooms and then she went to get her engineering counterpart, whom we would also be talking to for the next 90 minutes.

We set up the Flip video camera and unpacked our notebooks and paper and markers for the drawing exercise at the end. Mike (that's what I'll call him) came in with Melissa. He was much more reserved than she was, which was expected, but we got started and things were going great. They were playing off each other well—they both had different perspectives on the subject we were studying and that was coming out very well in the interview.

But 55 minutes into the session, we were completely interrupted by an angry guy slamming the door open and barging into our conference room. He knew we were doing a private interview in there, because the walls were glass, but he barged in just the same. He started yelling at Melissa and Mike—as if we wouldn't pay attention unless he used his outdoor voice. "We're meeting with [important company name] next door—let's go!" Who the hell was this guy? And how obnoxious for him to walk in on our meeting without knocking or excusing himself. He hadn't even made eye contact with us.

Melissa was taken aback. This other meeting wasn't even on her schedule, so she was a little confused, but she tried to handle it and excused herself to go talk to this lunatic. I stopped the Flip, and without prying into the details, tried to get a read on how important this meeting was and if we should start packing up to go. Mike just sat there silently, as if this behavior were completely normal and things would pass over soon. He didn't have any kind of reaction to the incident at all. We told him we could finish this at another time if Melissa weren't free—maybe over the phone or email. He just shrugged.

Melissa walked back into our formerly private room, was very apologetic, and said that we could continue, but she was obviously distracted. She was under the impression that we would just be another five minutes, and I told her that this was actually a 90-minute interview, so we still had 30 minutes to go, but we could hurry and wrap it up in 15. She paused for a moment, and we thought "OK, that's our cue. We'll leave and let you be." But Melissa said that Mike wasn't needed in the meeting after all, and he offered to stay and talk with us. So we plopped back down and said, "That would be great." Melissa apologized again for not realizing how long our meeting was supposed to be and promised to reply to questions over email instead. I gave her a hug as she left the room. She looked like she needed one. I gave her a sincere Gosh-I-hope-you-don't-get-fired-today "thank you." She left and went into the conference room adjacent to us, and we heard the call begin, because the walls didn't go all the way up to the ceiling.

With Melissa gone, we asked Mike the next question and realized we would probably spend no more than 10 more minutes with him. Not more than one minute later, as soon as we started to get comfortable again, the crazy guy came back and started yelling at Mike! "We rescheduled this for you—we need you on this call. If you don't come, we can't close this deal." Now we realized this *was* a bad situation. Mike casually said, "OK," got up to leave, and asked us to email him the questions.

They just left us in the conference room, all alone. We packed up our stuff and awkwardly made our way to the front door, none of us saying a word. We walked down the nondescript hallways in silence, making faces at each other to share our mutual feeling of "What the hell was that?" but we kept our cool and made it out of the building. On the way back to the car, the only thing I could do was apologize profusely to my designer and engineer. "I'm so sorry, guys, that has never happened to me before. I feel so icky. Usually, my interviews are a lot more professional than that, and people don't come in yelling at the people you are interviewing."

So we spent the car ride back pretending to barge into each others' interviews, laughing it off, and trying to regroup for the rest of the day.

Elaine Ann: I Thought My Client Was Going to Die

One of my most memorable research experiences was ten years ago in China. My Western client fainted in broad daylight in the middle of our Beijing field trip. We had completed field research work and were touring an exhibition. She just plopped on the floor without any previous sign that she had any health problems.

We called the ambulance, and a white van came along. There was nothing on it—no ambulance emergency lights, no oxygen equipment, no CPR equipment, only a stretcher. Not knowing what was wrong with my client's health, we (me, my colleagues and her co-workers) decided to take her to the hospital anyway.

Upon arriving at the hospital, we had to first pay for the ambulance fees in cash (this is China). Then the client was carried onto a hospital bed. I was caught in between cultures at that point as my client's Western co-workers were dubious about the medical standards in Chinese hospitals and refused an injection from the doctor; while the Chinese doctor was quite annoyed by the Westerners' attitude (reading their horrific facial expressions) and challenged them whether or not they really wanted to be helped after coming to the hospital. Meanwhile, I was trying to translate everything in both English and Mandarin, amidst all the chaos, trying not to offend either party (who couldn't communicate directly with each other).

Finally, the client's co-worker decided to take a risk with her boss's health rather than risk it with the Chinese hospital, so we had to shuttle the client back to the hotel instead. (We then discovered that five-star hotels usually have English-speaking travel doctors for emergencies—a handy tip for researchers doing field trips in China.) In the hotel elevator, my client fainted a second time, and we had to drag her off the elevator, along the corridors, and into her room like a dead fish.

My client finally became conscious again and luckily we found out that this was caused by a low blood sugar syndrome and happened all the time. All she needed was a piece of candy. We had to decline her request to visit the Great Wall the next day. I really wouldn't know how to carry her down from the Great Wall if she fainted on top of that, as it's a defense wall designed to make it difficult for invaders to climb even in ancient times!

Seriously, I would have made the national news if my client had died on our China research trip! Phew!

Ryan DeGorter: Enthusiasticus Interruptus

Our UX research team created a program called "Coffee with Customers" where we conducted interview sessions with our customers over a hot brew. It not only allowed us to take a step back from the daily grind, but also gave others in the organization a chance to be involved in the process. With this particular coffee and research session, I took along a product manager "Bob."

Prior to the coffee session, I walked Bob through the interview style, and provided him a rough sketch of how the interview would flow. Bob was particularly interested in gaining insight on how people used social applications, so I worked those into the discussion guide. The research session started at 10 a.m., so I picked Bob up at 9 a.m. to give ample time for one last review with him. I explained that I would like to be the one to lead the interview in order to maintain the flow of the discussion. However, if he had a question to ask, he should try to remember to start the question with Who, What, Why, How, or When.

It was a wintry day, and Bob and I arrived at the coffee shop shortly before 10 a.m. It was quite crowded as we did an initial scan for the participant "Kevin." A few minutes later, Kevin arrived. During introductions, it was clear that Kevin was a bit tentative about the session. When we were ordering coffee and muffins, it was difficult to start a conversation with him. Nevertheless, we found a table where we could sip our coffee and chat. Since Kevin was clearly nervous, I spent a little longer making small talk in hopes of trying to remove the awkwardness. We chatted about the weather, and how Waterloo (Ontario) never seems to get a proper winter anymore.

Before long, we had a stronger rapport with Kevin, so we dove right into the interview.

I started with questions like "Where did you buy your smartphone?" and "What was your thought process for choosing that one?" Kevin continued to open up and was providing us with good detailed information. He gave us very clear stories about why he chose that particular phone, what he enjoyed about it, as well as points of frustration. All this time my partner Bob was sipping on his slightly cooler coffee and taking it all in without writing any notes. It was as if this were his normal daily routine and this interview was like every other research session he had done before.

As we delved deeper into Kevin's usage patterns, we moved on to the topic of social applications. I asked Kevin to walk us through why he used Facebook and Twitter and asked him to show us how he did this on his smartphone. Bob shuffled his chair closer to Kevin so that he, too, could observe Kevin's actions. Kevin confidently swiped through the Twitter application, explaining his rationale for following certain friends. At this point, there was a sudden interruption, which caught both Kevin and me by surprise. Bob leaned in even closer to the device and pointed to the screen as if it were his own phone.

"Do you do it like this?" Bob asked. "Um ... I don't think so." Kevin replied hesitantly. Bob then suddenly grabbed his pen, hunched over the table, and with both arms on the desk, furiously wrote on a piece of paper, acting as if he needed to catch every word that was coming from Kevin's lips. It felt like everything was going into hyper speed, and I was no longer the pilot of this interview. I could not make out what Bob was actually writing, but he obviously had some specific answers that he needed to write down personally.

I tried to ease the tension that Bob's action had created, saying, "That's great that you use the application that way, what else do you do on this phone?" I tried to convey to Kevin that he was *not* being tested and that instead we were just seeking inspiration and under-standing. Unfortunately, Bob interrupted again and asked Kevin to navigate to another area of the application, asking "Do you do this?" type of questions while he clearly had specific answers he was looking for. This went on for another few minutes, despite my efforts to regain control of the interview by trying to rephrase Bob's ques-tions in a more open manner. My efforts were in vain, and I could see Kevin was shutting down and resorting to *yes* and *no* answers. I needed to act and act quickly.

"It looks like we need some refills. Why don't we take a short break?" I said in a desperate attempt to free Kevin from Bob's interrogation. I was lucky that Kevin needed to use the washroom, so I took the opportunity to speak to Bob in the coffee line. I reminded him that we had an audio device, so we did not have to write down any notes. I also addressed his interview style. I politely stated that I would be asking the questions during the remainder of the session, while making sure to address those items that he provided me with in the discussion guide. Bob took my concerns to heart and allowed me to complete the interview without interrupting. We never fully gained the openness back from Kevin, but overall, it was an inspiring session for both of us. As we shook Kevin's hand good-bye, I made a mental note, thinking "This is why those UX books encourage you to ask questions instead of your stakeholders."

In the field, you always have to be on your feet. A single participant can be tricky as you try and figure out their personality and what will help them feel comfortable enough to talk openly to you. Additionally, your colleague may also become too eager and sidetrack the session in order to get their questions answered, despite being told how they should approach the participant. When things go awry, you need to be able to stay calm and get the interview back on track. It was great that Bob realized his mistake during the break, and I will not let this experience prevent future colleagues from accompanying me during a session. However, I will definitely spend more time explaining to my colleague the importance of rapport and emphasizing the proper technique on how to ask participants questions so as not to overwhelm them.

Nicolas Nova: Do You Want Me to Act?

I remember a study I conducted that was set in a big shopping mall in France. We were there interviewing users of smartphones for an R&D project. The place was pretty standard, and we decided to sit in a fast food joint called "Quick," at the entrance of the mall (which means a lot of people were passing by). Given the focus of the project, we had to videotape the interviews and take pictures of the posture of the user. This meant that the presence of cameras was hard to hide and that passers-by couldn't avoid noticing them.

After four interviews, we started the fifth one, kind of tired after hours of discussions with informants. Right in the middle of this interview, my colleague and I saw a tall guy moving toward us with urgent haste, putting his two hands on the table, and screaming the following line: "I've just been released from prison, and I'm hungry! What are you guys up to? Are you in the video business? Do you want me to act? Or what?"

The size of the guy, his level of excitement, the face of our informant, and the people around us made the event very odd, as it stopped everything for a second or two. It's this sort of situation in which you have to behave yourself and avoid pissing off the nervous intruder, take care of the informant awkwardly paused in her description, and reassure the audience that was frowning at us. The guy seemed so energetic (after all, he'd just re-entered society), and he looked at the same time excited about a new opportunity *and* being a thug about to rob us of our devices. The "or what?" was said with so much hatred in his voice that we were a bit nervous.

We explained to the guy that we were interviewing someone, asking her about her perspective for a research project, and that he could be a participant later on. We were hoping that would be the end of it, a sort of way to make him understand that this was not the moment to chat with us.

Of course, he didn't seem convinced, or he simply didn't get it because he said, "Oh yes, I've got a friend in Marseille in the video industry. I know your stuff!" To which he added, "But why do you have so many telephones?" My colleague explained the project and that was the end of it. "Arf, I don't get it, I don't care, plus I'm hungry," and he left as fast as he had arrived a few minutes before.

Nothing really bad happened here, but it was awkward for us, a sort of break in our interview day, which actually readjusted our energy because we then completed three more afterwards!

Vanessa Pfafflin: DDoSed in Vegas

My company provides health- and wellness-based businesses with business management software centered on scheduling and point of sale. My colleague and I were visiting Las Vegas for a trade show and decided to tack on some field visits at a couple of our Vegas clients' businesses. We planned to help out at the trade show booth for two days and then do one day's worth of observational research before catching our flight back home. The first night we were in Vegas, we were notified that our company's computer system was experiencing an Internet-based attack known as DDoS[1] and our software was completely down for all 17,000 clients. Our sales people were panicked. The show was five days long, and we knew that it would be a really terrible week if they were unable to access the sales demos for the show if the server remained down.

Unfortunately, the attacks continued for two days before we were able to install a new firewall and switch to a different data mitigator. We humbly kept our booth up sans demos. By this time, our war-torn trade-show team had improvised with screenshots of the product. Some of our clients showed up at the booth—many of them offering reassuring words, while some met us with anger.

At the end of the second day, connections were restored. I contacted the two clients we had planned on visiting the following day, and asked if their sites were up and working properly. Both clients assured me that their systems were back up and running just fine, and said they were anticipating our visits.

The next morning, we visited our first client, a massage therapy business, and we were greeted warmly. We spent three hours onsite (mainly troubleshooting), and they thanked us with complimentary 60-minute massages! After two days on the DDoS battlefield, it was the best gift a girl could ask for.

Our next client was a 30-minute cab ride away. By this time in the day, the temperature was in the 100s, and we pushed through the wall of heat up the steps and into the lobby of the second business, a yoga studio. When we walked in, the girl at the front desk studied our business name embroidered on our shirts and said, "Oh you guys, you're on our shit list right now." We apologized on behalf of our company and offered to help in any way we could. The girl did not want to have anything to do with us. Our software outage had made the last two days at work so difficult for her that all she wanted to do was scream. I asked to speak with the manager, with whom I had been working to schedule the visit. After 30 incredibly uncomfortable minutes waiting for him in the lobby, we made the decision to leave.

---

1 A DDoS attack is a Distributed-Denial-of-Service attack. A technical definition is at http://rfld.me/DDosAttk

The reactions of our two clients were so dramatically different that my colleague and I were left feeling quite bewildered as we waited for our flight back home. In retrospect, I'm glad we decided to go forward with the visits. Although the visits turned into more PR than observational research, we felt good about showing up and offering our support. In this situation, external factors put a damper on our research and put us in some pretty uncomfortable situations. In one of the situations, we were presented with an opportunity to help, and in the other, we learned when it is best to just stop and walk away.

Elaine Fukuda: They Call Me Mister

I admit I don't have a lot of experience with children, but the opportunity to shadow a patient through an entire day's hospital visit was one not to pass up. The patient being 13 years old added another layer of consent and assent, a mythical ethnographic research unicorn of sorts.

The goal of shadowing was to understand the experience of the entire visit from start to finish, through multiple provider visits, labs, tests, and the waiting times in between. I met the patient and her mother as they were pulling into the parking garage, and the girl started the day with a scan. During the next two hours, this girl patiently laid in a claustrophobic tunnel, and did everything as asked, from changing positions ever so slightly, holding her breath for 30 seconds at a time, and breathing at a specific pace.

Having fasted since the previous evening, she was ready for lunch, but wanted to get everything done before their provider visit, so she and her mother decided to get a blood test done before lunch.

We arrived in the pediatrics department and her mother stood in line to check in while I joined the patient in the waiting area. After a few minutes, a volunteer came over for what I felt was a break in our somewhat awkward small talk.

The volunteer was a kind elderly man with a book cart offering free books for patients to take home. The patient, tired from the scan and possibly feeling out of place in the bright and cheerful pediatrics environment, shrugged and said there wasn't anything she liked. Determined, the volunteer took out a "magical coloring book," which colored itself with a flip of a page. She was still not impressed.

Then came the pièce de résistance. From the cart, the volunteer pulled out a heavy woven rope and introduced the patient to his friend, Mr. Stick. Mr. Stick had a magic ability, you see: with a grand gesture, he could become taut. In order to turn back into a rope, the patient was instructed to ask, "Mr. Stick, will you go down?"

The shade of red across the teen's face had long passed lobster, and she and I stared at each other in disbelief. Her mother was still in line across the way, and as the adult I felt responsible but conflicted on what to do. Surely the man had no idea what he was implying? Being a very good sport, she complied and sure enough Mr. Stick fell limp.

But the volunteer didn't stop there. He turned to me, holding the middle of Mr. Stick, now back in its rigid state. He asked me to tell Mr. Stick to go down, which I did. Nothing happened. The volunteer said I must say, "please," which I did. And again nothing happened. He then said, "I guess Mr. Stick doesn't go down if you're not a child."

"Hey, I think they're calling your name," I quickly said to the patient. And with that we escaped the somewhat creepy, but well-intentioned volunteer.

"That was awkward," she said.

It wasn't until after the blood test and during lunch that we were able to debrief and talk about the encounter with the volunteer. I was afraid her mother would be upset that I hadn't intervened sooner. She was shocked but laughed, wondering if someone could really be that clueless. As I started to explain what had happened, the patient (who had been sitting right next to the volunteer) intervened:

"No, its name was Mr. **Stiff**, not Stick."

Me: "Oooh, that's even weirder."

Mother: "I'm really curious how you're going to write this up."

Takeaways

- **It's OK to walk away, especially if you've tried everything.**
  Sometimes circumstances totally prevent you from accom-
  plishing your research objective. But trying and failing can
  be illustrative, whether it's about participants and aspects of
  their culture, or about how your organization is perceived, or
  even about this particular research venture. If nothing else, it's
  a chance to have a laugh. Knowing when to walk away (from
  anything, not just an interview) is a life skill and not something easily codified.[2]

- **Call a timeout.** When the interview (and the context in which
  the interview is happening) feels almost completely out of control, take a step back and readjust. You may take a pause ("Give
  me a moment, please.") when you feel unsettled, but a timeout
  is more extreme ("Let's all take a break for a few minutes."),
  and you shouldn't use this technique prematurely. By the same
  token, don't wait too long, such as when you are too frazzled to
  reflect and adapt.

- **Use the breaks you are given.** When external circumstances
  disrupt your flow, use that as an opportunity to readjust
  and reenergize.

---

2 In Kenny Rogers's Grammy award-winning song "The Gambler," the title
  character offers the narrator a great deal of life advice, including, "You've got
  to know when to hold 'em, know when to fold 'em, know when to walk away,
  know when to run." "The Gambler" never got down to the specifics, however.

- **The unexpected can reveal bold new truths.** One of the prized aspects of working in the field is that things happen that you weren't expecting but that reveal something powerful that you wouldn't have ever imagined to look for, as we saw in Gerry Gaffney's experience with Mr. W in Chapter 2, "Those Exasperating Participants." But sometimes the unexpected is just a monkey wrench you didn't ask for, such as the recently released and hungry prisoner. You probably won't know which is which, even with experience. It's a reminder of the importance of staying open.

- **Improvise.** This often is expressed as saying "yes, and … " to everything that comes your way. In research, you have to be more selective about what you say yes to. When you're in the field, think about improvising as working from a script that is being created on the fly. Of course, improvised performances don't always proceed gracefully and sometimes splutter to an awkward halt. Improvisers don't consider that a failure, and as a researcher, neither should you. These awkward moments can happen, despite doing everything "right." If the script you start with falls flat, you can start creating a new script, pivoting to a different conversation. You can build improv muscles by taking an improv class, especially one that is less focused on comedy and performance and more on improv as an approach for solving problems creatively.

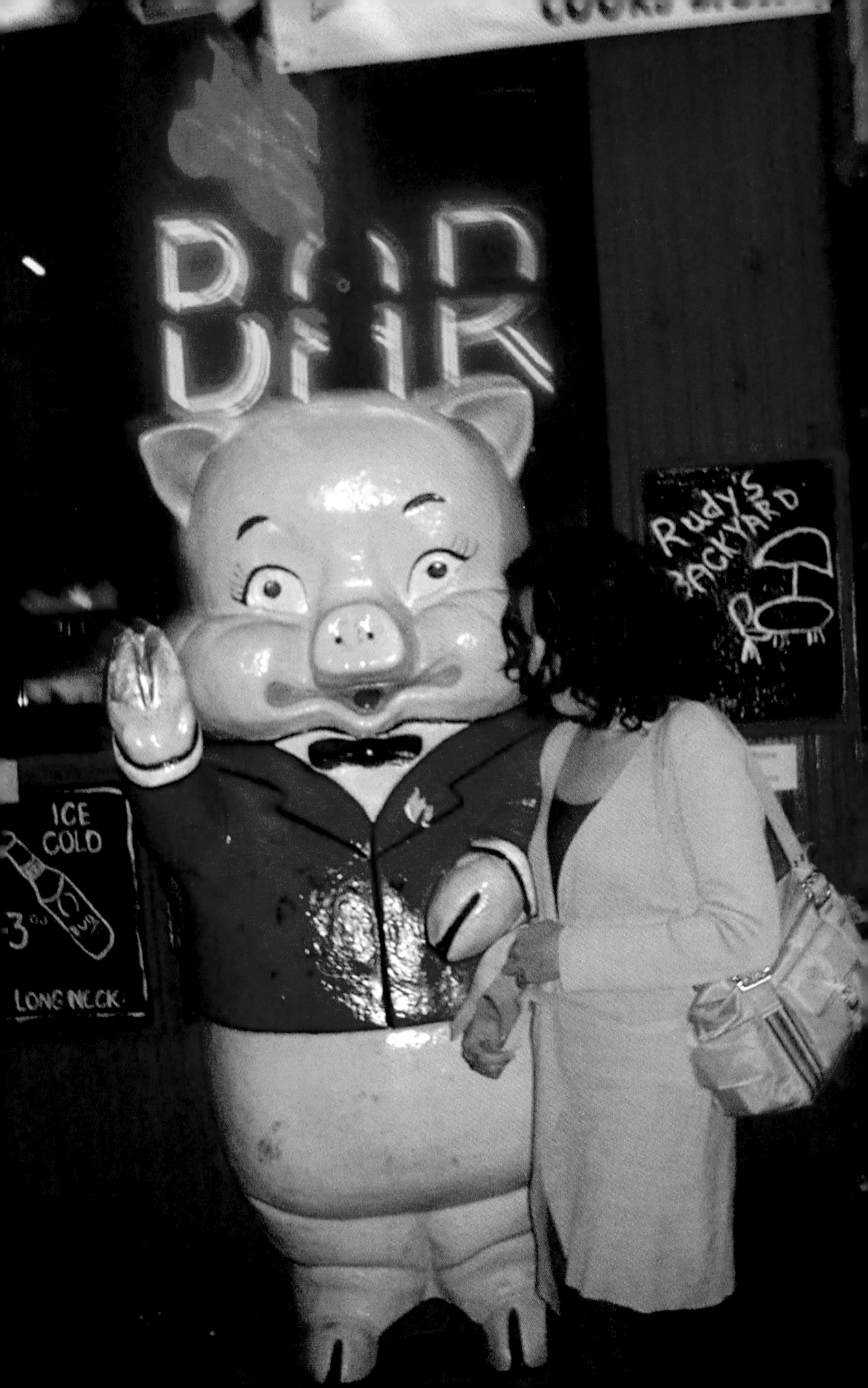
BAR
Rudy's BACKYARD
ICE COLD
LONG NECK

CHAPTER 4

Cracking the Code

Photo by Steve Portigal

In linguistics, *code-switching* refers to the (typically unconscious) practice of a speaker using multiple languages in a conversation. More popularly, the term acknowledges the ways that different ethnic, racial, and cultural groups adjust their speech patterns, word choices, and speaking mannerisms, depending on whom they are communicating with. In the first post to NPR's Code Switch blog,[1] Gene Demby explains code-switching as "the different spaces we each inhabit and the tensions of trying to navigate between them. In one sense, code-switching is about dialogue that spans cultures ... many of us subtly, reflexively change the way we express ourselves all the time. We're hop-scotching between different cultural and linguistic spaces and different parts of our own identities—sometimes within a single interaction."

Code-switching is an essential ingredient in research. Researchers themselves are not only code-switchers, but they are also code-breakers. The rich information that researchers seek goes beyond feature requests and verbalized preferences for one design over another. What research reveals is its own form of code, the cultural code ("the symbols and systems of meaning that are relevant to members of a particular culture"[2]). Skilled researchers work hard to uncover and decrypt those elusive codes, but sometimes there are cultural lines we don't even learn about until we cross them.

Researchers prepare as much as possible before going into the field, in order to be successful within whatever culture they are studying. Yet they are unlikely to fully understand the norms and rules of the culture before immersing themselves in it, and so once in the field, they must observe and adapt. Inevitably, researchers run into trouble when they uncover rules by breaking or bending them.

Researchers tend to emphasize that the work is about people and that success comes from building rapport with those people, but the truth is more complex—people are situated in a larger system, which we call the *environment* or the *ecosystem* or the *culture*. Some of the rules are basic and transactional (how to get in, how to get out), but others are more nuanced, and they require adaption, patience, and creativity.

---

1 http://rfld.me/CodeSw

2 "Cultural Codes—Who Holds the Key?: The Concept and Conduct of Evaluation in Central and Eastern Europe," by Jenny Hyatt and Helen Simons: http://rfld.me/CultCod

In this chapter, Gregory Cabrera's war story is about inadvertently bending, if not breaking, the rules in an actual war. David Hoard thinks he understands the cultural rules in a foreign country, but as he discovers, not at the level of fidelity necessary. Francoise Brun-Cottan faces suspicion from users who don't trust her efforts to document their work. Ari Nave breaks the culinary rules during his fieldwork. Chauncey Wilson arouses suspicion in a high-security environment. Jon Innes struggles to regain access in a secure technical site. Erik Moses fails to consider the functional constraints of his user's workplace. Each of them eventually cracks the cultural code, but not before the culture has a crack at them.

Gregory Cabrera: Taking Notes, Getting Detained (Sort of)

In the summer of 2010, when I first arrived at Kandahar Air Field, Afghanistan, I was unsure about how I would fit into a military culture. Just the fact that I was from California created a cognitive barrier for most of my military colleagues. Simply put, there were a lot of "don't ask, don't tell" jokes.

In any case, the first couple of weeks involved me playing catch-up and learning everything I could about the assigned area and region. I took copious notes all the time to help jog my memory and capture information that would come in handy later on. My hope was to refer back to these notes and re-create the picture that people were creating themselves based on scanty information.

PHOTO BY GREGORY CABRERA

In a war environment, you hear stories all the time, and you never know what is real or not. The jargon further complicates the situation and makes it difficult to navigate people, places, and things, all of which tend to be obscured in military code.

One evening, I was hanging around the base waiting to link up with my liaison, Mike. He was facilitating an introduction to a detachment commander whom I would work for over the next 12 months. Depending on how the meeting went, the commander would decide to bring me on board as a social scientist to work with him and his unit. I had tried to meet the commander earlier, but it was unclear where he was. His men told me he was busy in the port-a-john, but I think those guys were testing my wits. Long story short (and bathroom humor aside), we coordinated a meeting that night.

While I was waiting to link up with the commander, I noticed a large gathering of soldiers and civilians in an open area. Curious, I wondered if there was something I needed to be in the know about. There were approximately 50 or so people gathering around a projector to watch a PowerPoint presentation projected on the side of a wall. I assumed the crowd was too large to accommodate on this small base where work areas were tight. Doing this outside made no sense because fighter jets flew over and were so loud that it could cause permanent hearing damage. I thought to myself, "Well, since they are doing this presentation out in the open, the information can't be that sensitive. Surely taking a few notes couldn't hurt?"

This presentation took place right before I would be heading out into the field. As it started and I began writing things down, I started to feel more than a bit uneasy about what I was hearing. The gentleman started off by explaining that this fighting season was the bloodiest since 2007. A chart detailed the number of significant events (SIGACTS) and quantitative information about those killed in action, enemies killed in action, those wounded in action, improvised explosive devices found, indirect fire attacks, etc. Cough, ahem. I stopped myself at this point for a couple reasons.

First, I did not want to walk around with this information in my notebook in case I lost it and the enemy had eyes on this information. Second, I was sure this could come back to bite me somehow. I immediately became nervous because of what I already had written down. I started thinking to myself as well: I don't really need to be here.

PHOTO BY GREGORY CABRERA

As I started moving back, my actions caught the attention of a very attentive Sergeant Major. Typically, Sergeant Majors feed off opportunities to explode and make examples of others to reinforce the nature of their authority and rank. A strange civilian was the perfect feeding opportunity. Indeed, when I caught a glance at others in this crowd, no one else was taking notes or writing down information. "I'm dead," I thought to myself.

Before I knew it, this dude's eyes were piercing through me, and he pointed at me to stop moving as he came over to me. He yanked me out of the crowd and started barking questions at me, hands on his hips and head leaning forward: "What are you doing?! What were you writing?! Who do you work for?!" Frozen, I muttered something to the effect of "Uh, I, I'm just an analyst."

He took away my notebook and identification card and told me to follow him. The fact that I did not have a security badge did not help my case and only contributed to the uneasy feeling sitting in the pit of my stomach.

He sat me down in the operations center near the legal officer. He pointed at me and explained to others that he had caught me taking notes. He assigned a soldier to guard me while he figured out how to handle the situation. As I sat on the couch with another soldier staring coldly at me, I gazed around the operations center. There was a white board with a funny quote about strippers, an empty office with a blow-up doll in it (oddly enough!), and some metallic signs on the walls indicating this was football fan territory.

These guys were pretty laid back, but I had broken the social contract and had no idea what the repercussions would be. At this point, I wished I had just stayed in my sleeping quarters. A phone call to my liaison Mike was my get-out-of-jail-free card. The Sergeant Major explained the situation to him and the JAG (legal) officer.

The JAG officer called me into his office and explained to me the nature of note-taking in a sensitive environment. Even though the presentation was out in the open, my act of taking notes classified my entire notebook. He handed the notebook back to me, and I was on my way. I never saw the guy who detained me again. I wanted simply to get out, lick my wounds, and meet the commander who was waiting for me. The commander, who was not terribly impressed with my antics, laughed about my story. He decided to bring me on board on the spot despite my initial casting as a troublemaker. I like to think this gave me an edge, or maybe he saw value in having me around to take notes (ironically) and provide insight into the strange cultural environment he was about to encounter.

I shook off the embarrassment, but it was a story that got a few laughs in my organization. "Human terrain guy detained for taking notes." For me, it set the tone for the abrasiveness of military culture and reinforced my status as an outsider. I learned about the sensitivity of collecting information in a war environment and to be cautious about what I captured in field notes.

Jon Innes: Beware of Trapdoors

Early in my career, I helped a number of companies outside of the consumer space adopt methods from consumer design research for developing products sold to businesses. This is always a challenge because you have to explain to various people at the companies you visit what you want to do, and they typically think you are crazy.

In this case, my project involved trekking to companies around the United States to talk to telecom and networking geeks. My assignment was to study adoption barriers to Cisco's Voice over IP (VoIP) products, which meant physical phones, special servers to make them work like old-fashioned phones, and some software to set them up to do stuff like retrieving voice mail and dialing extensions or outside lines.

On this particular day, I was onsite at an Ivy League university. I had just spent several hours talking to telecom guys who clearly didn't like the idea of having to use some fancy networking gear or for that matter anything that was designed after Jim Morrison had died. I had just parked my stuff in the corner of a network operations center (NOC) that resembled NASA's Mission Control Center in preparation for a series of interviews with the staff there. Getting in the NOC was a major coup. Most organizations do not like outsiders in the NOC, especially outsiders with cameras taking notes.

About five minutes before my first interview with a NOC employee, I decided to make a run for the restroom. My time-zone-adjusting caffeine intake was taking its toll, and the person I was supposed to speak to had yet to arrive. I asked someone in the NOC for directions to the nearest restroom and walked down the hall, not thinking about much beyond the call of nature. I passed through several doors and got flashbacks of an old TV show called *Get Smart*[3] I watched in reruns as a kid.

---

3 https://youtu.be/ElqZms_SUjg?t=21s

I located my destination, but as I attempted to return to the NOC, I quickly realized I had a problem. In my haste, I'd left the secured zone of the NOC. The doors I passed through required a special badge to get back through. Worse yet, I'd left my bag with my ID and my notes of whom I was supposed to visit, and I couldn't remember the name of the person I was meeting with next.

While most companies make you sign in, I had not needed to that day. I had an escort from the IT group show me around, leaving me at each place for the time we agreed upon so that I could do the interviews. But now I'm in an unknown part of the building, with no idea how to get back to where I was, or even how to get out of the building I'm in. I didn't have my cell phone with me, and there was no one in the hallway to ask for help. Even if I did find someone, like a security guard or an employee, I realized it was going to be really hard to explain this. After what seemed like an eternity, I talked a passerby into helping me contact my escort from IT, who kindly helped me return to the NOC. I managed to gather some good insights there during the time I had left.

To this day, every time I'm doing a study in a corporate setting, I always hear the theme from *Get Smart* playing in my head as I walk down those hallways and my trusty laptop case is always on my shoulder.

David Hoard: Footloose

Researcher Chinami Inaishi and I were on a 10-day trip to Tokyo to interview kids and young adults about their video game usage. It was 1995 and the console wars[4] were in full effect. Chinami is Japanese, but had lived in the United States for many years. So she was the perfect local guide to help me understand the cultural nuances we were witnessing. She also helped us navigate the nearly impossible house numbering system[5] in Tokyo, where house 31 was next to number 6, which was next to 109. This echoed one theme of the trip: squeeze things in wherever you can find space for them. Every square inch will be utilized.

---

4 http://rfld.me/con-war

5 http://rfld.me/J-Addr

The visits were fascinating and enriching at each stop. We saw small beautiful homes with Western-style furniture next to Japanese Tatami rooms. We interviewed a young man with the smallest apartment ever, a tiny 8' × 8' space packed to the gills with Western-oriented magazines, blue jeans, skateboards, and a full-size surfboard (unused). The kids were impressive, with their beautiful calligraphy work and exacting toy collections. In all cases, no square inch of space was unused, and that made me rethink the design we were considering. A low, wide game console was perhaps out, replaced by a slim vertical unit that could fit in one of their densely packed bookcases.

PHOTO BY CHINAMI INAISHI

Before the trip, I had done my best to read up on Japanese culture and manners. There's no way to learn a culture from a book or two—my goal was simply to avoid making a big mistake. I practiced and practiced the few phrases I would need. (Chinami was doing simultaneous translation for 98% of it.) I knew my two-handed business card presentation technique,[6] and I nearly understood the rules for bowing.

We'd been through most of the visits, and so far, so good. All of the sessions had gone fairly well, and we were learning a lot. But then I did something bad. Something wrong.

---

6 http://rfld.me/JapnCrd

We had been visiting a house near the end of a train line, slightly out of the city-center. The session was over; it was time to pack up the camera and notes and head out. We were doing our now-normal good-bye ritual, trying to check off the right etiquette boxes. And then it happened: I misstepped. Near the front door, I stepped my sock foot just off the wood floor and onto the carpet. With one shoe on already. Unknown to me, I just violated important etiquette about where you must be (and must not be) when putting your shoes back on when you leave.

Instantly, the whole family erupted in hysterical laughter, with everyone pointing at me. Suddenly, I was in a mayday situation, with my manners in a dangerous nosedive. Confused, I did my best to get my shoes on as Chinami pulled me out the door and onto the street. She was like a commando extricating someone from an international hotspot.

"What was that?" I asked, once we were out on the street.

Chinami informed me that laughter (apparently hysterical laughter) was how the Japanese coped with a faux pas or embarrassing situation. Embarrassment was indeed what I had created, and I felt it, too. Intense embarrassment comes with a whole set of physical sensations. You're flushed, addled, and dazed. You've got great regret, but it's too late to fix it.

When we go out to do field research, we often feel we are going out to observe a strange species in its native habitat. We are the scientists, and they are the creatures to be documented. We go to great lengths to help them feel comfortable with our scientist-like presence. We feel like we are the smart ones.

But guess what? The *research participants* are in their native habitat, and are experts on their own lives. We the researchers are the weird aliens. We're the ones not getting their nuances. We're the ones who are sometimes worthy of mockery.

But it's all in a day's work when you're out doing research; you've got to be light on your feet. Every research session I've ever been on has been a dance to cover the material and sniff out insights right below the surface—all while you try to make everyone comfortable and keep the conversation flowing. It's that dance that makes it exciting; just try to keep your toes in the right place.

Francoise Brun-Cottan: Black Glances Cast Our Way

It was the winter of 1989. Members of Lucy Suchman's group at PARC embarked on a multi-year joint Steelcase/Xerox project to look at ground control operations of two airlines at San Jose airport. Airport management and each of the airlines' managements were "on board." The project would study ground control operations of each airline in the existing airport facilities and then follow them over to newly built facilities in a new structure.

We were going to look at the interplay of paper (manuals, computer printouts), voice (over-the-air, walkie-talkies, radio, and telephone), chalkboard and whiteboards, and direct visual observation (versus camera/video feeds) of planes pulling into and out of the gates and being cleaned, fueled, and having baggage loaded and unloaded.

The plan was to use basic ethnographic methods and techniques: interviewing, shadowing (inside and on the tarmac), audio and videotaping, still photography, and transcribing recordings in order to ... well, we weren't quite sure exactly what we'd come up with. But we wanted to find out what could be extracted using these methods in such a tech-heavy environment. We were betting that it would be informative, insightful, and valuable to everyone concerned. We hoped.

In 1989, technology had come a long way from the cameras and recorders that had to be moved about on dollies and trailers, but as portable as they were, the wonderful Panasonic video cameras were heavy and so were the VHS tapes and batteries. The little Sony audio tape recorders (about the thickness of a stack of 10 iPhones) were great for interviews, but miking a control room took hours. Syncing the mikes with the video was a cabalistic art, colorfully augmented by below-the-breath expletives.

The members of the airline ground crews had basically been informed by management that they were going to cooperate. In reality, that meant they were going to "tolerate" non-lingo, literate researchers climbing over their equipment whenever they weren't actually underfoot, being recorded for hours at a time (rather gleefully when crises were underway), and being followed around and asked question after question (further confirming the depth of the researchers' lack of common sense and basic knowledge) whenever there was a moment of downtime.

We did try to tell the crew what we thought we were doing. But saying that we wanted to understand their work practices, how they would change in new environments using new technologies, and how they made sense of their work and communications was not exactly revelatory. As a field, we're much better at doing that now, partly because we've also got lots more examples we can show to prospective participants about results of our work.

Viewing the videos made clear what some of the crew members stated directly, which is that they were deeply suspicious of what we would report about their actions to management. Anytime they deviated from protocol, or made mistakes, or seemed to be resting rather than doing some piece of work might be opportunities for management reprisals of one sort or another. Some people were openly, if politely, hostile. No one welcomed us. It was tough on participants and researchers alike. They always cooperated at some level; there was no point in antagonizing us (though some were pretty gruff).

It is known that after a time people seem to forget that cameras are rolling, even if those cameras are right in front of them and so are the researchers. Viewing the weeks of tapes gave us plenty of opportunities to see them cast black glances our way, or whisper something together and laugh at us. In their banter, we also learned about their home lives and romances and trials and aspirations. Sometimes that could let us congratulate them; sometimes our knowing was resented.

I don't remember exactly when it became clear to our team—maybe somewhere toward the end of our fieldwork—that the final report would be a two-hour videotape, which came to be known as *The Workplace Project*. We said our good-byes and appreciations on the last days of fieldwork. "Thanks," they said and (figuratively) "good riddance."

We made sure that copies of the tapes were made available to the crews at both airlines. We learned that the report was being used by the crews to convey to mid-management complexities about the work that the crew members had not been able to convey. They repeatedly mentioned the benefit of demonstrating how manuals misrepresented events and complicated the work rather than facilitating it. Although previously unacknowledged in the organization, our work highlighted their level of expertise in differentiating personal task-relevant details from the sonic soup of incoming streams of information.

Sometimes, you just have to stick with it, whatever "it" will turn out to be. And then, sometimes, you get to be thanked for revealing aspects of the work that the workers can't make visible. A few years ago, I was told that Steelcase still showed that video to visitors at their user-centered division. So, that's not too bad!

Ari Nave: Chicken Run

My very first field research was in the north of Ghana along the Volta River north of Keta Krachi, trying to unpack the usage rights and other factors that enable the sustainable use of a common pool resource (in defiance of the tragedy of the commons[7]).

The research was hard. I was isolated, lonely, and physically drained. No one in the village spoke English. They spoke primarily Ewe,[8] and I was communicating through an interpreter. I had a feeling that I was missing a lot of nuance and detail with the interpreter and had several discussions with him about my concern.

PHOTO BY ARI NAVE

---

7 Also see "The Myth of the Tragedy of the Commons": http://rfld.me/TrgCmm

8 http://rfld.me/EweLang

I was also sick as hell of eating fish stew with fufu (a starch made from cassava and plantain)[9] or gari (a fine flour made from cassava roots).[10] For one thing, it was spicy as hell ... so spicy that at every meal I had these convulsive hiccups. This hilarity may have endeared me to my host, but the diet was monotonous.

I had spotted guinea fowl wandering around the village. I asked my host family about it, and they just laughed and said they were wild animals.

So I set my mind to catch one. That evening I watched as the guinea fowl hopped up a tree in the village. They used the same tree each night and seemed to jump up in a predictable pattern.

The next evening I was prepared. I had a long string for my trap. I tied a slipknot on one end and placed the snare on a protrusion of the trunk that was chest-height, a pivotal step on their journey up the tree.

The string was about 50 feet long, and I ran the length straight to another tree that I hid behind.

The folks in the village just laughed at me, which they seemed to do with great frequency. But I was determined. Patiently, I waited.

As dusk fell, the fowl made their way up the tree. When the third bird was on the spot, I yanked as hard and fast as I could, while running in the opposite direction. And I had the little bastard. He flapped his wings, I reeled in the string, and soon I had a plump guinea fowl in my hands. My host and all the other villagers came running at the commotion and now stood with jaws agape as I proudly displayed my bird.

I asked my host to put the bird in a basket and put a big rock on top to keep it secure. It was too late to cook the bird so I ate my mind-altering hot fish stew but with a content mind, thinking about the fowl I was going to eat for dinner the next night.

I woke up refreshed and optimistic. I gathered up my notebook, camera, and tape recorder and headed out, but first stopped to gloat at my catch. To my dismay, it was gone. I shouted, and my host came running over. "He has escaped in the night," he explained by way of my interpreter. No way, I thought. The boulder was still on top of the

---

9 http://rfld.me/WutFufu

10 http://rfld.me/WutGari

basket. Someone stole my bird. When I voiced my opinion to him, he shook his head and simply repeated the claim.

That night, I executed my hunt again, with equal success. This time, a larger group came out to watch my escapades and were equally surprised both by my technique and success. Again, I placed the bird in the basket, this time adding another large rock on top.

The next morning, I woke with foreboding. I jumped out of bed and checked the basket. Stolen! I was pissed off. My host tried to placate me, but I was having none of it. Arrogantly, I told him that I was going to complain to the head of the village. My host shook his head. He waved to me to follow him.

We walked toward the center of the village where the elder lived, ironically where the guinea fowl often congregated. Before we reached his compound, my host swooped down and picked up a guinea fowl with his hands! Of course, I had tried this many times when I first got the notion to eat one, but ended up running around like a fool. He lifted the wing of the fowl and I could see a colored ribbon. "Each bird is owned by a family," he told me. "There are no wild birds here."

So I had captured a bird that was someone else's property. I was confused because he had told me earlier they were wild animals. In the end, it turned out that he never thought I would be able to capture one, nor did he understand why I wanted to capture one. When I explained that, while I loved the fish stew, I wanted to expand my eating horizons, he laughed. "Just buy one from the neighbor, and my daughter will cook it for you."

So that afternoon I bought a fat guinea fowl and the daughter of my host prepared the most delicious ground-nut stew with it. To this day, I crave that stew. It was unlike anything I had ever eaten before and better than anything I could have imagined.[11] Although, it was still insanely spicy.

I felt a bit idiotic about the entire episode, and it only reinforced to the folks in my village how odd I was. But it had one positive side effect. People realized how little I understood about even the basics of their lives, and they began to be much less assumptive about my state of knowledge.

---

11 A similar recipe is at http://rfld.me/ChkSup

Chauncey Wilson: Secrets, Security, and Contextual Inquiry

In the 1980s, I worked for about seven years at Digital Equipment Corporation (DEC) as a usability engineer. My group was led by John Whiteside, who pushed to make usability a serious discipline informed by metrics, fieldwork, and lab studies. The method of contextual inquiry was developed in our group by John, Karen Holtzblatt, Sandy Jones, and Dennis Wixon. We did a lot of fieldwork to refine our methods and inform product teams about how to improve their products.

During my tenure at DEC, I set up a set of interviews with a major client who must still go unnamed. The client did military research and used some of our products. I got clearance to interview people at the site with the caveat that all videos, tapes, and notes would be surrendered when I left. I would analyze the data at their site and do a presentation about my findings, leave all data, and not discuss any details of my interviews. I got to the site early in the morning and signed in at the front desk. In those days, we had 8mm video cameras as our primary tool for field interviews. I had permission from the senior security chief to videotape the screens and record sound for five different users of our DEC products. I started setting up my equipment for the first interview and about the time I got to mounting the video camera on a tripod, three really large security guards with weapons blocked the exit to the office and asked me what I was doing. "I'm here doing some research for DEC." Then they grabbed my equipment and took me to a holding area and proceeded to interrogate me. I said that I had sought permission and had an agreement with the chief security officer—but that agreement was not to be found.

My name had been on the visitor list, and the people I was interviewing vouched for me that I had set things up with them, but there was no clear approval for videotaping. I asked if they could contact their security chief, but he was on vacation in the Virgin Islands. While they called and left messages for him, I spent a few hours in the holding area (you might call it a "cell"), concerned that I might go to prison. Though it took a while, they did catch up with the security chief and took me back to the cube where I had started my setup and let me continue.

I spent a week at this site and noticed that the guards walked by and checked in on me a lot. Every night when I left during the week, they had me empty my pockets and remove every item from my briefcase. On Friday, I put together a report and presented it to an audience of very serious people who asked no questions. I left all the data, submitted to my final contraband search, and left the most bizarre field visit of my entire career.

Erik Moses: (Don't) Go Toward the Light

Not long ago, I was on a project where we were tasked with understanding current practices in BioPharma labs. Overall, the program was a huge success, and we uncovered critical new insights for our client, which is always rewarding. But that is not what this story is about. This story is about my iPad.

As a researcher, I admit to having a bad memory. I am a dedicated note-taker. I love my notes and can't do much without them. A few months before this, I had begun using the iPad as my main tool for data capture in the field, moving on from my old friend, the pen and paper.

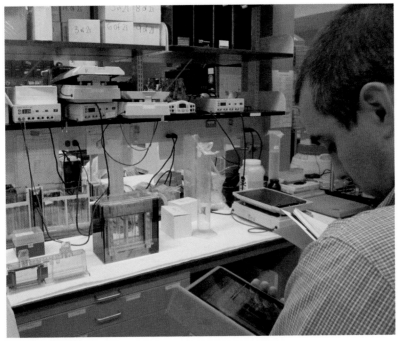

PHOTO BY ERIK MOSES

For one of our site visits, we were in the Midwest at a notable university lab. We were there for the day, courtesy of our client's long-standing relationship with this lab. That is to say, we were welcome guests. Part of the process we were observing involved a lab technician who was processing images in a darkroom. At one point during our visit, the PI (Principal Investigator), who was our client's main point of contact and with whom they had the relationship, invited our group into the darkroom to understand how the process continued in this environment. Of course, I took my iPad.

Our group piled into a cramped university darkroom to find not only the PI, but also a few other technicians from the lab processing portions of their project. It was dark in the darkroom, so the only thing I could see was the soft red glow of darkroom-specific lights.

The PI began the demonstration, while we tried not to impede the movements of everyone else in the darkroom. At some point, our participant said something very interesting that caught my attention. I thought, "Hey, this is a must-have insight I need to remember!" and so I opened the cover of my iPad.

Immediately, I hear a technician behind me exclaim "Wha-what? Oh, *great!*" While I now recall hearing this comment just like it was yesterday, at the time, I was so focused on capturing this important piece of information, I did not put together that the technician was referring to the blunder I had just made.

After noticing a tremendously bright light in this room of black, only then did my mind stitch together the visual information of the bright light with the auditory cue of the mumbled comment. In a matter of seconds, I realized what I had done.

While afterwards the PI ignored the incident and the session continued for the rest of the day without another incident, I felt horrible and was flustered for some time. Reflecting on it today, I still feel flustered. I like to imagine that I didn't mess up that technician's experiment that much, perhaps only by hours, but given what I know about that group and the process, in my heart, I know I ruined at least two days' worth of hard, time- and event-specific work.

Because of this incident, I am now very careful in the field, perhaps to the point of being overcautious, oftentimes wrapping my arms around my iPad to physically tell myself to be mindful of my actions. Learn from my experience: remember, don't (immediately) go toward the light!

Takeaways

- **Prepare for the experience of the interview.** You are already preparing for the conversation with your participant, but consider the entire experience. Reach out to whomever has granted you access in order to ask about logistics, dress code, or anything they think you might need to know when you get there.

- **Consider your assumption about the environment.** Again, you are prepared to forego your assumption about your participant, but don't forget the environment your participant is in.

- **Be present in your surroundings.** A lot of interviewing happens in the head, but don't forget about the body. You can remind yourself that you are in a physical environment by periodically noticing something about your body (say, how your shirt feels against your arm, or the position your foot is in). Keeping yourself grounded in your own body will help you be physically connected to the space you are in and support you in paying attention to the rules of the environment and, if necessary, adapting your actions to suit those rules.

- **Include the rich data from the environment in your analysis.** Context is king, after all, and the cultural code can provide a great deal of context about why a participant behaves a certain way or expresses a specific point of view.

- **Learn from your mistakes.** While this phrase typically implies that you should not make a mistake a second time, in this context, the point is that your mistakes and missteps may be ways to surface the cultural rules that wouldn't otherwise have been made explicit.

- **In corporate research, employees may fear they are being evaluated.** Be prepared to explain repeatedly that you are not evaluating their work or reporting on their job performance to management (assuming, of course, that this is true). Consider how your presence and your actions (e.g., your equipment, your demeanor, how you act with your research colleagues) may support or limit that impression.

CHAPTER 5

Gross, Yet Strangely Compelling

Photo by Steve Portigal

In an early episode of *The Simpsons*, Bart and a group of boys start watching a pornographic film. One child exclaims "Gross!" while another observes "Yet strangely compelling." This duality of attraction and repulsion is a driver behind schlocky horror films, children's edutainment, and certainly the stories we like to tell about user research.

Disgust, according to Daniel Kelly,[1] includes physical and emotional triggers that can be both universal (such as the smell of rotting garbage) or individual (such as the smell of certain foods). Disgust may have originally served as a protective mechanism (to keep us from ingesting something harmful), but it evolved to also serve a social function that establishes who *is* and who *is not* a member of a group. You can think about this in a tribal context, but also can find a familiar form in the way that vegetarians (for example) are connected.

Disgust can be managed, often through repeated exposure. Kelly points out that automatic mechanisms attenuate disgust, such as a mother developing a tolerance for her child's dirty diapers (but only from her child).[2] In an article about a forensic facility that stages simulated crime scenes with donated cadavers,[3] the scientists seek to manage their own revulsion and the revulsion of others by reminding themselves of the positive aspects of their work (such as the fact that the cadavers were donated and that they are in part fulfilling the wishes of the deceased). The author Alex Mar describes her own experience including the physical, emotional, social, and intellectual elements.

> At this point, I realize how quickly I've already adjusted to the
> shock of the dead: the trembling I felt in my stomach when
> they unzipped the bag has now mostly left me, and I've almost,
> almost stopped noticing the smell of cadaver. Though I'm not

---

1 Author of *Yuck! The Nature and Moral Significance of Disgust*: http://rfld.me/DisKell

2 Effectively mocked on *Seinfeld*, when Elaine's friend, a new mother enthuses "… but because it comes out of your baby, it smells good!" And sure, your parenting experience may differ. But there is science! "My Baby Doesn't Smell As Bad As Yours" in *Evolution and Human Behavior*: http://rfld.me/BabSmll

3 "Sky Burial: Excarnation in Texas": http://rfld.me/SkyBury

easily unsettled, to learn this about myself must count as a minor revelation: how rapidly I can recalibrate what repulses me—an ability taken for granted as a basic skill by many of the people in this room. I also realize that I've drawn a large measure of my comfort, my staving-off of total, primal panic, from the group reaction to rotting human flesh—which here, in this very particular place, remains one of calm appraisal.

Research has explored how disgust has moral and societal implications. A pair of studies published in 2009 showed that people who were more sensitive to disgust held more unfavorable attitudes toward gay people.[4] In another set of experiments, people who experienced disgust (through recalling a disgusting experience, or being in an unpleasant physical environment, or being exposed to an unpleasant smell—a "fart spray") were more morally judgmental (in one condition, reacting to a story of a man who failed to return a lost wallet).[5]

But we can rewire our own disgust. Psychologist and cognitive neuroscientist Rachel Herz explains that disgust and empathy are closely related emotions, both processed in the same part of the brain.[6] Deliberately choosing to act with empathy when we feel disgust will reduce that disgust.

In this chapter, researchers relate stories of fieldwork in unexpected, disgusting situations. They have no opportunity to prepare or rationalize. Yet, as their gorge rises, so does their empathy. Carla Borsoi, Prasad Kantamneni, Dennis Nordstrom, Brandon Satanek, and Gregory Cabrera each use their own discomfort as a data point, highlighting the difference between their own lifestyles and those of the people they are seeking to understand. Empathy turns out to be the counteragent for disgust.

---

4 "Disgust Sensitivity Predicts Intuitive Disapproval of Gays": http://rfld.me/GayJdge

5 "Disgust as Embodied Moral Judgment": http://rfld.me/MrlDisg

6 "Taking Control of Disgust": http://rfld.me/CtrlDisg

My small town doesn't offer home delivery of mail. Instead, we stop by the post office to retrieve mail from our boxes. Shortly after moving here, I began to notice a man sitting on the bench outside the post office. He would be there in any weather, at any time of day or evening. And he would just sit there, without a book, or a mobile phone, or anything. He would just look out from the bench. I would walk by him on my way into the post office and would have a strongly negative reaction. I couldn't identify the emotion, but I felt discomfort and a slight amount of anger.

In hindsight, I recognize that feeling as disgust, but at the time I couldn't imagine what was going on with this guy, and even as I saw other people greet him, I just felt this was somehow wrong. Once I got back in the car, I might make a joke. In fact, it reminded me of the 1990s television show *The Tom Green Show*, modeled after a talk show format, where a sidekick would always be sitting behind the set, holding a cup of coffee, just doing his thing, uncaring as to whether or not he was (literally) breaking the frame.

One day, perhaps sick of the frustration my own disgust brought out, I decided to say "hi" to the man. He said "hi" back, and that was it. But in that moment, my disgust was transformed. It cost me nothing to reach out with a greeting and in doing so, a weird situation became normal, even pleasurable. In the years since then, I always greet him and receive a return greeting, and I always get a small kick out of our exchange.

Carla Borsoi: A Dirty Diaper Sitting in the Mud

There is nothing like home research to challenge your notions of whether or not everyone lives like you. Earlier this year, we were doing research on how people used multiple devices (phones, tablets, and computers)—what they were doing with each, what they felt about each device, and how these were shared (or not). We were particularly focused on three audiences: Moms, Entertainment Junkies, and Earlier Adopters. Yes, in my world, we use Title Case to label our different audiences. At any rate, we picked three areas with high density for devices and plenty of each of these audiences in spades: NY, Seattle, and Austin.

I headed to Seattle in late March to meet with people and to talk to them about what they did. The first interviews went swimmingly: one Dad told us how he used his tablet to collect coupons, his computer to develop his Saturday shopping plan with coupons, and his phone to go through with his plan. He also told us about watching movies during lunch at work on his tablet. An Earlier Adopter told us how he obsessively followed tech news as he rode the bus. Good, I thought, these interviews were going really well. The Seattle weather was appropriately gray and rainy, but these folks lived in warm and welcoming homes. Normal, to me, at least, with the typical toys in the home with kids, the nice entertainment system, clean kitchens, and so on.

It was our last day of interviewing. The rain had been pouring down the night before, and I hoped it would hold off until I got to the airport at the end of the day. We were interviewing a young Mom who lived past Sea-Tac. I drove down pseudo-country roads and pulled up to the property for the interview. The driveway was full of mud. Thankfully, I was wearing wet weather boots. As I walked up with my colleagues to the front door, I passed a dirty diaper sitting in the mud. Huh, I thought. Their garbage probably got torn apart in the storm last night. The house was old, but that's how these things went. We were greeted by the young Mom and entered the house. Immediately, the stale smell of cigarettes and mildew hit my nose.

Uh-oh.

The Mom proved to be a bright, young woman, who tended bar a couple nights a week, while going to school and parenting the rest of the time. I looked down at the dirty table in front of me while we continued talking. She had some great insights about how she used her tablet (often on loan to her parents who would watch the kids), how critical her phone was to keeping in touch, and how her computer was there as she worked on projects for school. However, the smell assaulted my senses. I felt my two colleagues shifting in their seats, covering coughs. Our interview was scheduled for two and a half to three hours, but after about 45 minutes, I knew I wouldn't be able to handle it much longer. Someone asked if anyone had more questions. I quickly spoke up "Nope, think we're good." No one disagreed.

We walked out the door, and I noticed more garbage outside—but breathed in the sweet, clean air. I realized that as researchers we occupy a place of privilege. People allow us into their homes, without embarrassment or shame. This is their life. They allow us to see a window into it. People often participate in research for the chance to earn a little cash. This woman had spoken of how much they had saved to be able to rent this small, mildewed space. It reminded me that I have a lot of advantages that other people don't. It's a reminder that when we're creating products, we're doing it not just for some sexy, early adopter, but for real people who are just trying to make ends meet and get started with their life. It also reminded me to go home and wash down the walls of our stairwell, covered in grime.

Prasad Kantamneni: Skin in the Game

I was visiting an informant's home with a couple of colleagues to observe her trying to find information on the Internet.

Things were great—until she opened the door. The first thing we noticed was that the carpet had a lot of pink confetti on it. The confetti seemed to be everywhere. Then things turned scary when we realized that the confetti was skin—lots of it! The informant had shed most of her outer layer of skin.

At this point, all of us were worried that we would catch something. I knew my colleagues did not want to continue with the visit, but I didn't want to be disrespectful by canceling the visit without a valid reason. So I made the call to continue.

To give my colleagues an out, I asked them to record the interview— which gave them an excuse to keep standing. I then proceeded to ask her about the kinds of information she looked for online. She mentioned that, among other things, she sometimes researched her medical condition. At which point, I asked her to do what she would normally do when researching the condition. As she searched for the information, all of us were equally involved, trying to read if the disease were communicable!

Once we realized that the disease was not communicable, we were able to get past our mental block and proceed with the interview.

This is one visit none of us were likely to forget any time soon.

Dennis Nordstrom: Negotiating Between Sympathy and Empathy

Whenever we conduct design research, our aim is to gain empathy for our target audience. Through empathy, we enable ourselves to bring together our imagination and creativity as a way to develop a better tomorrow.

This was exactly our goal when our team was designing for people who were chronically ill. We were conducting research in major U.S. cities, and we were about to finish up our interviews in Philadelphia. We were preparing ourselves for the next participant and knew from our recruiter that she was a woman in her early sixties living on her own. Everything else about her was for us to find out.

As we walked up to her door, we were talking amongst ourselves about how inspiring it had been to actually meet all these participants and to hear about how they had overcome the major life changes that came with being diagnosed with lifestyle diseases such as diabetes, high blood pressure, heart conditions, or even chronic liver diseases.

We knocked on her door and heard a voice behind the door invite us in. We walked inside, and the first thing we noticed was the smell. It was extremely pungent, to say the least. It was the smell of old urine and vomit mixed with rotten wood and mildew. I saw a figure slowly emerging from the hall. Her arthritis was so awful that she could barely walk. Her dog was walking right next to her cane. It was an older dog, blind in one eye and with several teeth missing. It tried to bark at us, but the poor thing could barely make a sound. Besides the dog, our participant had about nine cats living in her house.

She came over and greeted us, and we introduced ourselves and thanked her for her hospitality. She offered us something to drink, but her condition was so bad that she needed help with getting the drinks out of her refrigerator and onto the table.

From the moment we sat down, we had cats crawling all over us. They were extremely curious and wanted lots of attention. One cat even laid down flat on my notebook, so that I would pay attention to it. It became clear to us that all manual note-taking was out of the question. None of us were able to write anything down.

We all sat there mesmerized as she told us her story. She was currently working as a part-time schoolteacher. She needed the health insurance and not working was unfortunately not an option for her. Over the last few years, she had been diagnosed with arthritis, diabetes, and high blood pressure. Her arthritis had gotten quite severe, and she was often unable to do much around the house.

As we sat there listening to her, I noticed a dry raspy sound. I looked to my side and saw that her dog was vomiting on the rug. Our participant paused and looked at her dog. She told us that as he had gotten older, he had become incontinent and would often get sick as well. As soon as she said this, the smell made perfect sense. Due to her illness, she was unable to clean up after her dog and cats, and over time it had all just been sitting there causing her rug and walls to slowly deteriorate.

I looked at my teammates, and sympathy was written all over their faces. They felt for our participant. A few minutes later, sympathy turned into empathy as she showed us some pictures hanging on her walls. One of the pictures showed her with some very official-looking people, in a very official-looking place. We were quite surprised when she told us that she used to be involved in peace negotiations between Israel and Palestine during the seventies. With the realization that this woman had not always been in pain and unable to get drinks out of her fridge, we were filled with an overwhelming feeling of empathy. She used to be a strong and assertive woman, who had had the misfortune of getting seriously ill.

At that moment, it became perfectly clear: this was something that could happen to any one of us.

Our newly gained empathy became a powerful catalyst for design ideas, and for the rest of the project, no team discussion happened without at least one mention of this woman.

Brandon Satanek: CATastrophe

I'll never forget the sight of that poor kitten munching on a cockroach. Our mission was relatively simple. Being employed by a large computer peripheral maker, we were to interview small businesses to see how they were using our products. The visit that brisk winter morning was to a costume rental shop that also did some tailoring. Upon entering the store, we were greeted with a smell, which, if called *pungent,* would be a kind and generous description. The owners, well, they must have had very large hearts.

I am actually a cat person (maybe it's their independence I admire). So the presence of a gaggle of feline friends could have been a welcome sight. But unfortunately, I don't think the owners were up to the task of caring for that many cats. In 2012 terminology, they would now be referred to as "hoarders." This was not a well-heeled, venture capital–rich setting; the building had a raw plywood floor, and the employees were doing the best they could to make a go of it. However, that flooring clearly did not help the smell-retention factor for animals that have periodic bladder control issues.

In many ways, the visit was worthwhile. As might be predicted, their computer system was not the latest, and it was good to see the struggles they had installing our software because of it. But, once that installation was underway, we experienced perhaps the slowest moving progress bar known in existence. Or maybe it just felt that way. Minutes drifted by before another column of pixels filled. It could have been the fumes playing tricks on my eyes, but I swear I saw that progress bar move backward on occasion.

My teammate and I began to develop various coping mechanisms. At first, we would periodically take breaths using the tops of our shirts as a crude filtering system. We were able to pull this off because we had positioned ourselves outside of the main office area and outside of view. Later, we began to make excuses for trips out to the car for supplies (aka fresh air). How were they to know we really weren't low on batteries or videotape? Unfortunately, the moderator was not so lucky and remained stuck with the participant. Yes, I do feel guilty about that.

Our minds drifted, and I began to wonder why anyone would actually leave clothes for mending there; perhaps their skills or prices were amazing. It was around this time when another creature joined the party. A cockroach skittered across the floor. A kitten gave chase. It did not end well for either, in my opinion. My teammate made that face which looked like she was gagging at the sight. Maybe this was just for effect ... but maybe not.

The visit ended uneventfully once the product was finally functional. In reality, I escaped with an interesting story and some clothes that needed freshening by the cold breeze entering my car during the drive home. I'm not so certain if those cats had a similarly good fate.

Gregory Cabrera: Biting Off More Than I Can Chew

In Afghanistan, hosts treat their guests as a gift from God. One of the principles of Pashtunwali—the way of the Pashtun—is hospitality, and a host must protect and treat his guests with the highest form of respect in order to preserve his cultural identity. An interview in Afghanistan is not a one-hour/gift-card-honorarium/thank-you-for-playing experience. Rather, it is a large chunk of your day, 4–5 cups of chai and maybe a meal if you are a welcomed kind of interview. This was apparent from my first interview in Afghanistan.

After my interview with the local police chief in northern Kandahar, I was treated to a cultural meal with my interviewee and another soldier. The soldier worked closely as an advisor and assisted me with the introduction to the interview. The police chief was a proud host, and he asked his men to prepare a special meal for us. As our interview came to a close, the men began rolling out mats, bringing in dishes, and placing large pieces of flat bread on the floor for us to consume. Typically, in this rural area, meals were eaten by hand from shared plates while sitting on the floor.

A typical meal consisted of rice, animal fat, and a vegetable. Meat was consumed on occasion, usually to impress a powerful individual. This meal consisted of okra cooked in animal fat with rice and naan (or flat bread). "A nice treat," I thought to myself, and a great opportunity to understand the cadences of daily life over a cultural meal.

The soldier who was working with me raved about the okra, telling me how good it was and that the local police grew it in the back of the building in a small garden. Sweet!

Ready to dig in, I grabbed a piece of naan and ripped it into a smaller, user-friendly piece. I took one bite and immediately noticed a strange and somewhat hairy texture. Attempting to be as inconspicuous as possible, I moved my head to the side and pushed it out with my tongue. I examined it and noticed what appeared to be a lock of animal hair, dark brown and gray, either from a rodent or canine. In Afghan culture, dogs are considered unclean and are not welcomed inside the home. Although part of me wished it was from a dog and not a rat, I pushed forward and avoided embarrassing my host. I moved on to the rice. The okra did not look very appetizing, so I tried to avoid eating it. However, my host asked why I was only eating rice, and the soldier next to me said I had to try it because it was so tasty. Oh, all right! I dove in. I ate until I was full, and concurred that the okra tasted great in the goat fat.

PHOTO BY GREGORY CABRERA

Making small talk, I thanked the police chief and his men for the food and chai. We talked about security challenges for the district and government, and some next steps in increasing the security bubble through checkpoints and army forces. This was good information that I could use for my analysis. As we said our good-byes and thanked our guest for his warm hospitality, I walked outside of his compound and the soldier pointed at the garden where the okra was being grown.

The small plot looked somewhat haphazard, not incredibly well maintained. I thought nothing of it until the soldier walked away, and I saw a young man walk toward the okra, squat, and urinate on the small plot of okra. Great, he was urinating on the okra they were using for human consumption!

Perhaps, the most valuable lesson I learned was to stick to the rice. In this context, I was able to share firsthand the lived experience of Afghan policemen and how they generated hospitality with whatever they had, despite it forcing me to sacrifice my bowel system and notions of cleanliness of my home country. If I had raised the issue or appeared disgusted, I would have risked losing the relationship and opportunities for future interviews while offending my host in the process. I wonder at what point do researchers draw the line when cultural experiences make us too uncomfortable or even sick? How do researchers cope with experiences that test the limits of cultural sensitivity?

Takeaways

- **If you know that your research will expose you to disgust triggers, desensitize yourself by exposure to those triggers.** If you can't see and smell them for real, look at pictures. If you can't find pictures, imagine the triggers as vividly as possible.

- *Acting* **empathetically reduces disgust.** In non-research situations, offer to help someone you feel uncomfortable with and that will reduce your discomfort, possibly empowering you for future research.

- *Thinking* **empathetically reduces disgust.** In the field, you may not be able to explicitly help them. (As we discuss in Chapter 9, "People Taking Care of People," managing that boundary can be its own challenge.) However, you can remind yourself that your objective in doing this fieldwork is to help them. Reframe the overall experience by identifying what is good about the participant's context and about your situation.

- **This too shall pass (or to put it less gently, "suck it up.")** Your discomfort is temporary and will end when the interview ends. Your participant, however, will remain in that environment. Reminding yourself of their permanent situation (versus your temporary one) can amplify your feelings of empathy.

- **Identify and manage limits.** You may take a break, and you may politely ask to remove a trigger. Specifics will vary, but if you can ask a participant to turn on lights or lower the volume on the TV, you can ask them to open a window or shift the location of the interview.

- **Celebrate your encounter with reality.** People who make products and services dwell in magically aspirational narratives about their customers. Experiencing the grit empowers you to help them understand the actual context they are designing for.

- **Remember that disgust is individual.** Shift team roles on the fly if another person in the field is more easily able to manage something that you find challenging.

CHAPTER 6

Not Safe
for Work

Photo by Steve Portigal

N SFW is an initialism that stands for *not safe for work*. It's typically used to mark Internet content (such as an email or a blog post) to alert prospective viewers that the content may be inappropriate for the workplace. Cultural norms and employee policies broadly establish what is and isn't acceptable, and the adoption of the NSFW tag is a signifier of that sensitivity.

Typically, NSFW is used to address material outside the scope of one's work. Researchers have to deal with situations where the content of their work is not safe for work. This conflict is a pernicious one—the researcher is charged with capturing the details of the real world and bringing them back into the organization, but doing so risks a human resources violation. Some companies are forced to develop a way to handle this. At Rackspace, a Texas-based company that manages and hosts websites for other companies, customer service representatives (who have opted in to this assignment) don a passerby-protecting Mexican sombrero when viewing customer's "adult entertainment" websites on their monitors!

Even if the rules of the organization will allow researchers to share this material, they still have to navigate the reactions of their colleagues, clients, and stakeholders. In the 1990s, I worked at an agency that consulted on a range of products, including medical technologies. We would have a weekly staff meeting to review the status of all of our projects, and any time the medical projects involved bodily functions, this meeting contained embarrassed snickers and puns that would make a 5-year-old roll his eyes. (Phrases like "things are looking up" and "... in the end ..." give you the basic idea.) I used to wonder how our clients—let alone our users—would feel that we couldn't even talk about their very real problems—the ones we were supposedly trying to "innovate" on—without a modicum of maturity. Of course, humor has its role in putting people at ease, but this juvenilia was the extent of the conversation and served only to reinforce the distance between us and the problem space. And so in that type of environment, researchers may modify what they share because of concern over distracting the audience.

As researchers, we bridge the conference room and the user's world. Taken out of the context of the interview, people may judge or react disproportionately to the "weirdness" of people's self-presentation. Some researchers actively manage what they share because they fear their message won't be heard. Internal politics vary, but generally

I hope that a gentle confrontation ("yes, *these* are our customers!") can help create a learning moment for the rest of the organization.

While interviewing the owner of a handmade corset business, my client and I took a tour of his facility. For some reason we weren't able to ask about, he had a rather impressive hardcore pornography showroom, with some astonishing posters advertising the brands he carried. Sadly, we were asked to turn off the video camera in that room. I say *sadly* because, well, I don't know exactly why, perhaps it was an interesting fieldwork moment to go from discussing the business operations (and the craft, quality, and health benefits of their products) to the surprise of this particular presentation, and it just seemed as if that's exactly what we were there to document.

I don't know what my client's feelings were as we walked through this room, but she exhibited calm and comfort. That served her well as we moved into the corset showroom and our participant eagerly offered for her to try on one of his corsets. She cheerfully agreed, and I continued to video and take pictures. The tightened corset (over her clothes) emphasized her figure dramatically (more than I presume she would choose), and this appeared to be the effect our participant was aiming for. And then my client pointedly asked, "Wouldn't you like to try one on as well, Steve?" to which I, of course, agreed. Our participant was willing to strap me in, although he seemed less enthusiastic, but my client and I were cheerful and engaged throughout the experience.

None of this was relevant to the reporting, but we immediately shared the story and the photographs with the rest of the team, and it actually served as a bonding moment for all parties. My client and I trusted each other and were able to separate ourselves from whatever unsavory (and unsafe for work) dynamics were going on with the participant. It was important to the field experience that we both participated fully and that included trying on the corset. And doing so seemed to neutralize any discomfort that she might have felt.

In this chapter, Rachel Wong finds real data in a participant over-share, and Debbie Mrazek catches the eye of a male participant. Kelly Braun and Carol Rossi keep their colleagues in mind as they run interference between what they are seeing and what the camera lens is picking up. Each of these researchers finds a way to negotiate the boundary between what may be appropriate in one context and what may be appropriate in another. That very effort is bound to yield insights of its own.

When the Work Itself Isn't Safe for Work

David Bloxsom
Owner, Villains IA & UX Design

"What do you do?"

"I work for a company that streams gay porn."

Depending on my audience, it was either a sure-fire conversation killer or the ultimate icebreaker. Gay audiences wanted to know how I could get anything done staring at pornography all day.

Because porn is so controversial, there's an assumption that the industry is all sex and drugs and no morals or standards. After all, you've already broken one taboo, so why not go all the way?

The boring reality is that no business would survive in that type of environment for long. I'm not naive enough to say that those elements don't exist in the industry. But most studios are more concerned with 1099s and model consent forms than lines of coke and all-night orgies. And the added scrutiny that porn studios are under forces them to be even more diligent than most other industries, with stringent documentation requirements for proof-of-age, consent, and STD status.

There was a rule that all locations involved in filming, production, or distribution had to maintain complete documentation for all the movies they handled. The government changed this rule so that only the "main office" had to maintain these documents. To celebrate, we had a "pizza and shredding" party where we all got together and destroyed the personal data of over 50,000 performers.

Even though it's often more conventional, working on the other side of the camera has its own set of rules and guidelines.

We made sure that any potential hire was aware of the content we worked with and what their potential exposure might be. Because we were a small studio, we didn't have the luxury of being able to have separate spaces for production and office support. This meant that our secretary might see a box cover or our accountant might overhear a graphic conversation about a shoot. You think your open office plan sucks: let me tell you stories about what it was like sitting near the editing department.

Although we worked in a porn-friendly environment, we would have visitors—someone's relative, mixed crowd parties, OSHA inspectors—who forced us to "de-porn." This would mean hiding DVD cases, removing film posters, and being more diligent about what was on our monitors. I used to joke that, at my job, you got in trouble for *not* watching porn.

We did all our shooting off-site. This reduced our risk of violating health and safety regulations. It also limited exposure to the most sensitive part of our business to those employees who were specifically hired for it. If models were in the office for business meetings, they kept their clothes on. We scheduled in-person auditions outside of business hours, and they only involved nudity, never performance. Online dating sites aren't the only place people try to use fake photos.

Setting expectations and controlling employee exposure to the content made it clear that, although we made porn, we were a professional office and not a porn theater. It also reduced the risk of a sexual harassment or hostile work environment lawsuit. And it changed the context of the material from "entertainment" to "product." But it was still porn, and there was no way we could completely remove the emotional impact.

One of my direct reports was a straight guy just out of college. He digitized the content and did quality control. This job involved scanning through every movie and spot-checking sections. Even after years of exposure, there were times when he came into my office asking to go home early because of something traumatizing. Knowing he could pass on content that made him uncomfortable gave him control over his work environment.

Working in an industry considered immoral forced us to be even more professional, not less. We had to be more diligent about following the law; more conscientious about the work environment we created; and more communicative with our employees. And above all, we had to create and enforce an attitude where we viewed the content as a job and not as something to enjoy, at least not during business hours.

Rachel Wong: Subject Matter May Be Inappropriate

I was working at a design firm, doing a quick photo diary study. The user segment we were studying were young X-Games-types, e.g., risk-takers and thrill-seekers. We were trying to get inspired by their mindset and approach to life. This was back in the days when Polaroids were commonly used in fieldwork studies for people to document aspects of their lives in context. We gave each participant a photo diary kit, which included a Polaroid camera, film, and prompts on sticker labels. They were asked to use the prompts to inspire their picture taking and then to affix the corresponding prompts to each photo. The prompts for this study were open-to-interpretation statements like: "This gets me excited" or "This is a relief."

One of the guys I'd recruited for the study was an acquaintance whom I'll call Bobby—a shy, sweet, young guy big into skating. I was so happy he agreed to participate. A week later, I dropped by his house to pick up his completed kit. "Thanks, it was fun," he said earnestly, and I gave him his incentive and thanked him.

As soon as I was home, I reviewed Bobby's photo diary and did a double take when I saw that for one of the photos Bobby had documented himself in the act of sex with an anonymous partner, associated with the prompt: "This feels good." For a Polaroid, the photo had an impressive amount of detail, in close-up, no less.

Suffice to say, this was much different than the average photo diary entry and shocked and entertained my project team the whole next morning. As I posted all the photo diary responses in a large grid on foamcore, I struggled with whether to include the illicit photo in my display. We ended up turning it around, and then hiding it away when the client came for a meeting.

But when I think about it now, I realize Bobby was communicating something about his life approach that was powerful and honest. It makes me wonder how much we edit our study participants' responses in light of work appropriateness, and even how many of our study participants edit their own responses, shielding their most real opinions in exchange for what they think we want to hear.

So, thank you, Bobby, for giving me an ounce of your truth, although I wasn't really equipped to handle it. And I'm glad it was fun.

Debbie Mrazek: Sometimes Ignorance Is Bliss

Many years ago, when international "day in the life" visits were not common in my company, I led a study to better understand technology usage in typical homes.

As a U.S.-based team, when we spent time with a European family, we typically included a translator and local researcher on the team. Each visit started with getting to know the family over a meal that we brought with us. We then toured the home and divided into smaller groups in order to spend focused time with each family member.

During a visit with an upscale German family, I was interviewing the very friendly and excited older teenage son. He very enthusiastically showed me every gadget, software program, and PC trick he knew. He was constantly trying to impress me with his technical skills and knowledge, speaking in a mixture of German and English. The interpreter did her best to help me understand the boy's key points, but I continued to notice that both she and the local researcher were exchanging knowing smiles. Eventually, the mother joined us and graciously suggested that the son had "bothered the poor girl" (me) enough, and we should join the rest of the family for coffee.

During our post-visit debrief, it was revealed that the interpreter was strategically *not* translating some of the boy's most blatantly flirtatious comments, leaving me unaware that this was even happening. While typically I think the translation should be unbiased and accurate, in this case, her careful filtering was a good thing. It allowed me to focus on watching how he used the technology … but it did make for plenty of teasing from my colleagues during the rest of the trip!

Kelly Braun: Pictures Are Language Independent

At eBay, we did a lot of field visits. We were always overprepared with checklists, allergy meds, extra batteries, and everything else we could think of for the unexpected.

For this particular study, we were interviewing people who had bought large equipment on eBay. This visit was to a store that had purchased a giant Xerox machine that had been used by big corporations. This video store specialized in Chinese language videos.

I perused the movies as we got set up. Some were American movies that I recognized by the pictures, even though the titles were in Chinese. Others were films made specifically for the Chinese-speaking audience.

We interviewed the owner, and he told us about the amazing deal he got on the machine and when we asked if we could see it he said, "Sure, it's in the back." No problem, we had extension cords for the video camera.

I took the camera off the tripod and followed the store owner and my co-researcher into the tiny back office. I couldn't really get a good shot of the Xerox machine from the door, so I went inside and around the machine to get a better angle. At this point, the owner said, "Oh, I forgot. This is where the porn videos are … but don't worry—they are all in Chinese."

I looked up and the side of the room I was now facing with my video camera rolling was filled with porn—all with Chinese titles, but let's just say it really didn't matter that the titles were in Chinese because … well, a picture is worth a thousand words, regardless of the language!

My co-researcher just soldiered on asking questions and all I could think of was "Wow, am I supposed to film this guy with all the frolicking nakedness on the video covers behind him?"

Lesson learned: Make sure that you know how to override the auto-focus on your camera!

Carol Rossi: Driving Force

Since Edmunds.com (where I work) is an auto website, we spend a lot of time hearing about how people shop for cars. A couple of years ago, we ran a shop-along study where we conducted in-home interviews to both understand car shopping behavior and simultaneously screen people we might want to go with on test drives to dealerships. I always take someone else with me when running interviews—a designer, product manager, exec, etc.—so they get firsthand exposure to real car shoppers.

This time, I had the head of editorial with me. The Edmunds editorial team has a long-term fleet of cars, so they can write about car ownership. My colleague told me that he would drive, and we took one of the fleet cars. We met in the lobby, and he walked us over to a $100,000 red BMW. It's not what I typically show up in to interview somebody who is probably shopping for a Honda.

The interview was in Hollywood, and although it's only 10 miles from our office, this was LA so we drove up Santa Monica Blvd. for almost an hour. We found the address, and it wasn't in the best part of Hollywood. There we were with this six-figure car. Eventually, we found a parking spot that looked relatively safe and walked to the building.

We used the callbox and were buzzed into the building. We looked for the apartment and realized it was in the basement. We were greeted by our interviewee, a middle-aged guy who was described on the screener as a self-employed writer (like much of the population of Hollywood). The apartment was the tiniest living space. It really looked more like a one-car garage. The air was stuffy, there was a unique odor that was somewhere between musty and dusty, and there were no windows open and no A/C, with carpet that had probably never been cleaned. I started to hope that the allergy attack I was sure was coming would happen after we were finished. The apartment was overstuffed with piles of papers (screenplays?), VHS tapes, and posters of independent movies (including one with a woman in bondage gear whom we later discovered was his wife). Although we'd normally want to capture anything descriptive of the scene, to avoid distracting the product team who would watch the video later, we had to position the camera to keep the poster out of the shot.

We were chatting, and after a few minutes, our interviewee's 35-year-old wife came out with a baby. The wife was some kind of Hungarian model (think of a European version of Gisele Bündchen). The guy turned out to be really nice, educated, and articulate, but also clearly not at all someone likely to test drive a car at a dealership. Basically, he hated cars, rode his bike everywhere, was trying to get off the grid but needed a car now that there was a baby, and said he would buy some used car that's parked on the street with a sign in the window.

Was this interview all for naught? From the first moment through the end, I wasn't sure. You always learn something new, so even though this guy did not meet our criteria for people likely to buy a car at a dealership, we certainly got exposure to a type of shopper we knew theoretically existed but hadn't yet encountered ("the eccentric car hater").

I've seen homes like this (and worse), but after the interview we walked outside and my colleague couldn't unload fast enough. He'd never seen a living situation like that. In rapid succession, he declared (out of concern for our safety) "When we first walked in, I thought it was a trap—I was looking for a way out" but then (out of concern for the child's health) repeated several times "They have a baby in there!" And then he began to express his concern for my safety "Do you go on these interviews alone? You take a guy with you, right?"

After this emotional decompression, we jumped back into the ostentatious Beemer and drove down Santa Monica Blvd., away from the unknowns of the ethnographer's life to the predictable comfort of our office ... until the next interview.

Takeaways

- **Know your organizational rules and culture.** Don't be afraid to challenge them, but protect yourself. This might require a conversation with HR or a manager.

- **Provide trigger warnings.** Before showing controversial content, give people fair warning and the opportunity to opt out. This is both compassionate and empowering and may create the type of learning moments that transgressive field data can inspire.

- **Just because your work involves a [body part] doesn't mean you have to act like one.** If you are exposed to something uncomfortable, find a way to deal with your discomfort that doesn't marginalize your user, the problem, your data, or your colleagues.

- **Do fieldwork in teams.** If you are uncomfortable, your colleague may be able to take some of the weight off you. A shared awkwardness has a better chance of being a funny story than a solitary, embarrassing one.

- **Consider the range of controversial content that you may encounter, beyond sexual and sexist.** You may see or hear racism, intolerance for LGBTQ, or evidence of drug use. Be aware that others may be more sensitive to these issues than you.

CHAPTER 7

To Live Outside the Law, You Must Be Honest

Photo by Steve Portigal

C onsider these three scenarios. For each of them, ask yourself, what would you do?

- You learn about a high-ticket item (such as a car or a computer) that you suspect was stolen.

- You learn about a high-ticket item that you know is stolen.

- You see someone in the process of stealing a high-ticket item.

Responses to this question will vary by individual, but you might factor in elements such as risks and consequences for yourself and for others, expectations for the efficacy of your actions, and general ethical principles. Of course, responses to this question are not good predictors of the action one would actually take. Research shows that we rate our past behavior as more ethical than it was, and we predict our future behavior to be more ethical than what we actually will do.[1] Nonetheless, it serves as a baseline.

Now consider those scenarios again, but with the additional context that each of these happen while you are in the field, conducting research with your participant. Your responses may or may not change, but your process for determining a response will. As researchers, we must consider our responsibility to our participant. If you only learned about illegal activity because you asked a research participant to trust you, then how does that change things? What are your obligations to accuracy in your research? To your stakeholders and clients? And to "the authorities"?

The ICC/ESOMAR International Code on Market and Social Research (the ethics document from a global organization for market research) emphasizes the researcher's duty to the privacy of participants and states that the researcher must avoid doing anything that exposes participants to harm. The American Anthropological Association's *Handbook on Ethical Issues in Anthropology* (a misnomer or overstatement of what a "handbook" might do as it offers more actual stories than proscriptions) has a case study in which an anthropologist witnesses a murder and documents the entire experience in her field notes.[2] The village deals with the matter through a "death payment," but when the police come, knowing she will be

---

1 *The Ethical Mirage: A Temporal Explanation as to Why We Aren't as Ethical as We Think We Are*: http://rfld.me/EthMrg
2 "Case 3: Witness to Murder": http://rfld.me/WitMurd

questioned, she has to decide whether to destroy or conceal her field notes (spoiler: she conceals them).

Reading the AAA handbook helps us to understand that this is a complex, long-standing issue in social science fieldwork, where notable situations include fleeing a cockfight broken up by the police[3] or embedding in the world of crack dealers in East Harlem.[4]

Social science ethics crossed into the mainstream with the controversy over Alice Goffman.[5] The sociologist, who is white, spent six years living in an African-American neighborhood in Philadelphia. After publishing her thesis *On the Run: Fugitive Life in an American City* to great acclaim, a number of challenges emerged, ranging from her complicity in illegal activities (she describes driving her armed informant as they search for someone who is suspected of killing his friend) to verifiability (she burned her field notes) to privilege.

As researchers, we have to consider the consequences of observing and of documenting—even if we are permitted or even invited to do so. And there are consequences that can impact our participant (and their extended community), our clients, our research, and even our careers. Lena Blackstock, Andrew Muir Wood, Susan Wilhite, Raffaele Boiano, and Nick Bowmast face less sensational circumstances than Goffman, Geertz et al., but face the same ethical questions, nonetheless.

Lena Blackstock: The Researcher and the Banana Thief

While getting my Master of Design Ethnography at the University of Dundee, I was able to dive headfirst into full-on ethnographic research projects with actual clients. We were asked to do research on self-service usage in Scotland. After the first few interviews and shop-alongs, I met one of my last participants in a nearby coffee shop. Initially, she was only going to do an interview, but then agreed to

---

3 "Deep Play: Notes on the Balinese Cockfight" by Clifford Geertz. When Geertz and his wife join villagers in hiding from the police, this common experience facilitates their access to interview and observe the villagers going forward. http://rfld.me/Geertzply

4 *In Search of Respect: Selling Crack in El Barrio* by Philippe Bourgois

5 There are copious articles about this, but the *New York Times Magazine* is a reasonable overview. http://rfld.me/ALGoff

also do a shop-along the next day. She offered to invite her roommate along, which was especially interesting as I was trying to understand more about how groups use self-service technology. I jumped at this opportunity.

I met the participant and her roommate in front of a large grocery store in town, and we moved through the aisles as they stocked up on groceries for the week. They were sharing a cart throughout the shopping trip, but when we came up to the self-service checkout area, they each took out their groceries and separated them on the checkout counter. They each managed to navigate through the self-service process without any major glitches (aside from the occasional "unexpected item in bagging area"), even with the loose fruits and vegetables they had to weigh and scan.

PHOTO BY LENA BLACKSTOCK

After the shopping trip, we went back to their home, and I wrapped up with a few informal questions to get feedback on their experience during this shopping trip. As I was finishing my last questions, my participant's roommate said something that caught me by surprise. I asked them about any issues they may have encountered during scanning or weighing items at the checkout, and almost as an afterthought, she mentioned: "Well no, not really, but you can trick those machines when you weigh stuff, you know? For example, when I buy bananas, like today, I hold them up a bit when I weigh them so that the machine only charges for a smaller amount than it really is."

Yikes! Had I just gotten myself into one of those ethical dilemmas that we had talked about in Uni? I had unintentionally captured a self-service banana thief. In one of our previous modules, we had conversations about dealing with these dilemmas, but those were theories. I was now in the real position of having to make a choice as a researcher. Should I stay true to the data and include the information in the final report for the client, even if I didn't directly observe it or ask for it? And what about the fact that the banana thief wasn't even the actual participant whom I had recruited, but her roommate? Does that make a difference? On the off chance that the client wanted more details on this fact, how would I handle this? Surely, I had to hold true to the confidentiality agreement with the participants, right? Or should I just leave that one tiny bit of information out of the report? Was it really that important to the report if I weren't asking for it? But what if this piece of information, which got me into this conundrum in the first place, was actually pertinent to the research project and addressed some of the client's challenges and pain points?

In addition to these concerns, I also had to work within the University Ethical Guidelines. And as an ethnographer-in-training, I had to make a decision on how to handle this information. Not only this one time, but from this point forward if I was going to go out into the world and work as a researcher. I realized this was as good a time as any to ask myself: What kind of values am I going to live by as a researcher?

In this case, I chose to include the findings in my report and stay true to what I had observed. I made a very conscious decision that no matter what, I would not share the confidential information of my participant. In the end, the client was happy to hear the "real story," as it confirmed some of the security issues of this technology that they were suspecting. Now, would I make this same decision the exact same way in a project today? I can't say. Many factors play into the decisions we make as researchers and often, we have to rely on some sort of gut feeling. But encountering this situation at the beginning of my "life as an ethno," forced me to internalize the challenges and to make a choice.

Most research projects have their own version of a "banana thief," an unexpected observation or something overheard, something that challenges your approach, your assumptions, and your moral code for conducting research.

In the end, my chance encounter with the self-service banana thief didn't provide me with answers for future encounters, but did present me with a first instance to ask myself questions and to begin shaping my personal approach to research. And that is a good start.

Andrew Muir Wood: Victims of the Killer Insight

I'm an in-house researcher for a start-up that is building a business information research tool used by financial and professional services customers. We try to spend as much time as possible in the offices of our user base, which takes a hefty bit of negotiation to arrange. Design research for enterprise software is tough. You need to wade through non-disclosure agreements, busy timetables, and corporate politics to get to the right people, and even then, it's hard to know if you're hearing the company policy rather than the real motivations behind behaviors and decisions.

On one such project, after months of preparatory meetings, emails, and reschedules, I found myself midway through a series of inter-view and observation sessions, at the desk of a busy corporate participant, a target user of our tool.

Toward the end of the session, he was walking me through his typical processes. As I watched and took notes, he exported a list of companies by logging into an online research tool (not ours) using an email address that was clearly from a competitor of his current employer. I didn't ask, but I was pretty sure this email address—and associated access to this tool—was from his old job (a cursory LinkedIn check confirmed this fact later).

I was astonished that he made no attempt to conceal this action. "There's no way of doing this quickly with our current tools," he explained unapologetically. The data he exported would save his whole team days of manually trawling for that information.

Rejoice! The hallowed "killer insight"! He had just demonstrated a concrete need, across his whole team, for functionality that our research tool did really well. For a short moment, I basked in the glory of my discovery. But wait. Crap. This was complicated. For three reasons.

First, the conditions for getting access to this participant. A firm "suggestion" from his boss's boss was the reason I could get two hours of his time. In exchange, I was required to report my findings back to the senior manager at the end of the research. This stakeholder would be very influential in the adoption of our product across the organization, so we needed to build a business case out of pain points, time-consuming tasks, and makeshift solutions. However, what was the company policy on using tools from a previous job? Maybe they were fine with it. Everyone does that, right? In regulated industries? I was not so sure.

Second, I'd put a lot of effort into gaining the trust of the participant. Although he'd been briefed on what to expect, he was initially uncomfortable about my being there and offered up terse, monosyllabic answers to my questions. I used a questioning technique that explored the proportion of time he spent using the skills that he was hired for versus other types of tasks. Paying attention to his frustration with the company's tools and bureaucratic processes helped to build empathy, and he began to open up. I felt that it wouldn't be fair (and I don't believe it was my job) to report him to his bosses for trying to save time for his whole team.

And, finally, most perplexingly, with this makeshift solution in place, this participant and his team would not currently perceive this usually monotonous task as a problem and neither would their bosses. There would be no way to explain the need the research had uncovered without revealing specifically what I had observed.

What do you do when you have an insight but can't reveal where it came from? Turns out, you go to Scotland. I needed to find someone else in the same business who had the same problem but solved it in a different way. Fortunately, the company had a completely separate regional office in the bonnie braes of Scotland, and I was able to speak with participants in similar roles there. I observed how *they* went about gathering company data and found that they had more legitimate, but far more time-consuming solutions, which helped me build my case, without mentioning "password-gate."

This situation occurs in business software design research because of the fuzzy distinction between uncovering insights about a customer for product development purposes and using those same insights to sell your solution to them. You don't always get access to users at all, so I was lucky to be able to speak to enough of them to explore the problem fully and build a case for adopting our research tool, without getting anyone in trouble!

Susan Wilhite: The Trust Dance

My employer called with the assignment: get a feel for a range of consumer Wi-Fi behaviors. The wilder, the more intense, *the riskier*, the better. It was fieldwork in New York City, this time shadowing a Dominican guy in Queens. Tech-edgy and as proud of his gamer laptop as greasy dudes are about their hotrods. It was early July, and I was there to get his story: the what, how, where, when, and why—especially the *why*. The hacked, the black-marketed, the legacy, and the shiny new, and all the numerous income streams. In New York, like everywhere, everyday life is all the drama you need.

First, he had advised me *not* to stay in a crummy, cockroach-infested hotel close to his place. No, I should stay in Manhattan, and he would come get me, each and every day. And so he did. At 9 a.m., he was at my hotel lobby on the upper West Side to escort me on three subway lines and a bus. His place was his aunt's and cousin's house on a street Archie Bunker might have lived on. At 21, he is *el hombre de la casa*.

I saw the situation right away—I needed his cooperation if only to get back and forth every day, and I couldn't tell how long his reliability would last. He had not a clue what ethnography was. So I said to him, "For the next three days, you're working for me. We're pretending we're making a documentary about you and your devices. We'll talk, and you show me stuff to illustrate your points." He bought it. We were in business.

He made a lanyard to wear my digital recorder around his neck, to better capture his comments over the *loud* air conditioner while he ran Lara Croft through a troublesome Tomb Raider level. We sat at the white, wrought-iron patio table out back and discussed his take on every wireless access point in the neighborhood. He demonstrated how he invented ringtones in the front room to sell at one joint or another. He was a boxer on the side—he knew people.

One morning, he packed his virus-infested hotrod laptop, and we headed to Brooklyn. He had talked his techie friend into occasionally wiping his hard drive. "Good as new," he said. By this time, I've spent seven-something hours a day with him, and not every moment pertained to the research. In fact, it was exhausting for both of us to keep running in this acting-out demo mode. So it was a relief to watch other parts of his life, which sometimes exposed incidental intersections into the topic at hand. But, on the way to Brooklyn, he dropped hints about how to walk and look at people to avoid unwanted attention.

His techie friend, it turned out, was less than thrilled about the risks of wiping a friend's laptop hard drive. Maybe there were even some unspoken debts and favors between them—I don't know. I played along. The afternoon was getting long, and the air was heavy. This was his mother's house, and the grand furniture and stuffed curio cabinet suggested it had been in the family for a few generations.

Apparently, the subject of our being there must have been carefully broached. Veering into distracting topics gave the two parties a chance to modulate the tension. So they asked about me. They were also looking for reasons to impart respect onto me and maybe be OK with my being female and older than them. I said more about myself than was strictly professional, but that was the point—they wanted to know I was OK, I'm human; I'm not taking advantage of them. I could be trusted. A few revelations about my video game background conveyed cred that seemed to lubricate the moment; I was one of them, at least for now. Shortly thereafter, it came to light that while I was in no danger, there was something illegal about the hard-drive-wiping thing.

The trust dance subsided, and now we huddled in a back room. A fluorescent bulb lit the scene, and the New York Transit Authority roared outside the barred window now and again. What I witnessed was ripe stuff, but being there, in that room, with these people, in that moment, was mildly warped. But this was the real deal, the reason we do research. I avoided shooting the illegal parts, even as I avoided endorsing their actions. I was all objectivity on the inside and going partly native on the outside. Mission accomplished, the "high five" was caught on camera, and my guy and I were outta there.

There are ethical lines in what ethnographers do. To be really committed, it's tough, though, to pull back, to play it safe. To be willing to seek humanity is to push boundaries.

I had meant to bring his gratuity with me on the last day, and I just plain forgot. His girlfriend came along with us back to my hotel. As we rode one line, then another, I sensed no distrust in my intentions, but they were a little anxious. They watched as I signed the traveler's checks at a grand old table off the lobby, and then they turned out toward a hot night in the vicinity of 89th and Amsterdam. Upstairs, after downloading the media, recharging batteries, and writing field notes, it's 10 p.m.—time for dinner and a drink. It's my birthday.

Raffaele Boiano: The Enemy Employee

In 2010, I was hired by a research firm to investigate the work climate at a government-owned company in Milan. I was pretty confident in ethnographic research. After two easy interviews, I went to meet Mr. N, a long-time employee with an office in a separate building.

It was a hot July day, and I was uncomfortable in my suit (mandated by the assigned dress code for this research). The front door to the building was open and as soon as I entered, I realized that I was alone on this floor. From the lobby, I phoned Mr. N to be sure that I was in the right building. He answered and in a calm and kind voice said that he had noticed me from his window and asked me if I could wait a few minutes while he finished something up.

I sat on a sofa by the entrance, totally alone, looking toward the elevator and the stairs. After 20 minutes, he phoned me, "Hey, Mr. Boiano, I'm available now, can you come find me on the second floor?" I felt a bit neglected. It wasn't very polite to ask me to look for him in an empty building, without knowing where to go. But the weird part of the experience was still to come.

I went up to the second floor and then down the hallway on the left. After passing a few rooms, I called out his name loudly, but there was no answer. After passing a few more rooms, I met a man and asked him to show me where I could find Mr. N. He took a seat: he was Mr. N.

"Mr. Boiano, I'm glad to meet you. But you surprised me, and I'm never surprised. You took the hallway on the left, the darkest one. Most people simply decide to go toward the light; it seems that they prefer their comfort zone." I was totally astonished by his first sentence. I was in front of him, shaking hands, without being able to think of any response. He was middle-aged, tall, and skinny, and I was a bit scared.

Mr. N asked me, "So you're here to interview me? This is going to be an evaluation?"

"No way!" I responded, trying to set the right context and expectations. "I'm working for Company X. We're involved in a change management project, and we're starting from the employee's point of view. We really think that people like you know a lot about the company, and we want to include your thoughts in the organization design process." I felt pretty awkward, but I continued my introduction. "If you sign the privacy agreement, we can start the interview. I ask for your consent to record the interview, so that I will be able to listen carefully to your answers without being distracted right now by note taking."

He interrupted me, "Let's agree to this: I will tell you the truth about our company if you don't record our interview. And I'll sign your papers." I was inexperienced, and the possibility of hearing an awful truth was very tempting, so I accepted and took out the notebook from my backpack.

My first question was open ended, "Let's talk about your role and daily work routine. What can you tell me about that?" He waited more than 10 seconds and then said, "Nothing. I can't say anything about my daily routine because my days are empty. The only activity I do is open the door every morning and close it every afternoon." I was trained to wait 15 seconds before asking a follow-up question, so I waited while he looked at me unwaveringly.

"Can you describe your role at the company?" I asked.

"I'm a fossil, a dinosaur. At least they want me to feel like that. I was hired just 15 years ago as a middle manager. The boss assigned me an impossible project and after two years, I was the only one who was punished for the project failure. Have you ever been a scapegoat?"

I gazed at him intently. I was willing to wait as long as it took because I had the feeling that he wanted to talk.

"No, you never have!" he said. "You're young. You're still convinced that the world can be fixed. Even this company. The truth is different. Look at me. They have buried me in this empty building. I'm the only one on these two floors. The weirdo in the cage. And I've tried to resist. I was close to a nervous breakdown. But I've got an escape strategy: I don't do anything. Anything at all. They might say I'm stealing my salary, but I'm proud of it."

While half of my thoughts were empathic, I was also thinking about several ethical dilemmas: Should I leave this interview out of the analysis and report? Would I be able to protect his privacy if I used his quotations? What kind of value was I providing for my client if I kept silent about Mr. N's theft of taxpayer resources?

I froze, locked in my thoughts. I lost focus and eye contact with the interviewee. He was going to get up. I had the feeling that the interview was over.

Almost stammering, I asked, "Who are *they*?"

That was the beginning of a new interview. He felt my interest in his story, and his anger decreased. My acceptance of his confession created a sort of shared understanding, and then we had a chance to talk a lot about the organization's problems. In the end, I decided to completely omit the first part of the interview from the research report. Fortunately, I was able to include a lot of insights from the second part of the interview.

Nick Bowmast: Diary Studies at Motorway Speed

"I could show you something that might blow your mind right now if you wanna see it?"

I'm a few minutes into an in-home interview following a diary study, and Aaron (the research participant) was about to show me the first of two dodgy behaviors that would test my field research "poker face."

"Yeah, sure, why not" I say, trying to mask my intrigue at this enticing invitation.

The study was for a cable TV company that had bravely commissioned this fieldwork to "paint a picture of the viewing landscape" and uncover how people were getting their stuff to watch, legally or not. In this case, it turned out to be mostly the latter, and moderating my surprise and intrigue became a bit of a challenge.

Camera rolling, I followed him down the hall, ready to have my mind blown. He showed me the utility room, where home brewing, laundry, and terabytes of piracy occurred. With great pride, Aaron demonstrated his dedicated, highly sophisticated (and very much illegal) torrent server, running a very impressive, underground but open-source software managing his library of hundreds of films, TV series, and so on. He was quite open about the fact it was illegal, as he described how the server fetched, then collated pirated content, all set up so that it couldn't be tracked back to him.

The guy was a hacker. He showed me how he had "jailbroken" his Apple TV and installed a new UI over the top via his Raspberry Pi so he could browse and play all the content on the screen in the next room. I was impressed, and super interested. Considering the extent of the setup—and its dodginess—I was well aware that my client would hate this guy. He posed a significant challenge to their business. But I couldn't give any of this away to this piracy pioneer. I had to keep an ace poker face.

One golden rule during interviews is never to express surprise or judgment in response to things people say or do. I felt like I had done a pretty good job of maintaining a neutral response, rather than the "Holy crap" or even "'How can I get that setup at my house?" thoughts that were jostling for front of mind. This was good practice for what came next, as pirating content wasn't the only law this guy broke.

For the 10 days before the interview, Aaron had kept a video diary, taking short clips to capture the moment in the different contexts of which he was watching stuff. After the excitement of discovering his piracy exploits, we started watching some of these clips. Most of them were selfies, shot while viewing something. In the first couple of clips, he was on the couch soaking up the latest crime investigation series he'd torrented, as you do. A few clips later, the video took me by surprise. Yes, it was a selfie, but rather than a living room backdrop, it had the blur of motorway traffic. He was filming while driving. Yep. Then he turned the camera to the traffic ahead, then down to the dash, where his smartphone was leaning on the speedometer. Aaron was driving at 60 kph, while filming a selfie of himself watching a video.

The clip was about two minutes long, and in it he explained that as a tradesman driving between jobs he was often doing this while cruising on the motorway. As he's filming (and driving, and watching) he explained: "Yeah, driving is really unproductive, so I find time while I'm driving to do a few YouTube searches. It's something I do a lot of, and this time it's a clip about a new recipe for my next home brew."

PHOTO BY BOWMAST CONSULTING

As we were watching the clip, I put on my best poker face, trying not to appear surprised in any way at this. In the video, he continued, "It's probably not the most responsible thing to do, but it's *my* downtime, and I like to keep up with my hobbies."

Nope, nothing to see here officer.

To be fair, none of these things really "blew my mind." When you're there—in context—it's easy to identify with what motivates these behaviors, and these motivations were what I needed to convey to my client.

Suspending judgment in the moment turned out to be a snap compared to my clients' suspending theirs when I played back a video profile of Aaron. Initial laughs began to verge on outrage at the law-breaking aspects of the selfie-driving clips, with some discussion of calling the police.

In terms of the project, my clients started to dismiss the behavior as a one-off, and I thought this was a backfire, but the authenticity of the footage was hard to ignore, and this helped me get my clients past their judgments of Aaron's behavior to understand his motivation. The fact that he'd gone to such lengths—knowingly breaking the law—to access this content in a way that suited him was a pivotal insight in the project.

Now all participants in my diary studies sign a waiver. They are responsible for their own actions during the study, but I also promise that they will remain anonymous, as I don't want them to edit their behavior. No officer, nothing to see here either.

Takeaways

- **Identify where your obligations lie.** Even if you can't generalize how to resolve conflicting obligations, at least be conversant with the elements to consider. These can include legal elements, as well as ethical, and should factor in the different players: clients, employers, participants, and so on.

- **Think of ethics as a conversation, not a specification.** While these situations are far from unique in the history of field-work, they are sufficiently diverse and complex that people continue to discuss and debate them. Examining choices you have made and considering choices you might make in the future will help prepare you. When different parties have different priorities for conflicting obligations, it's important to surface and discuss those.

- **Build a support network.** IDEO's *The Little Book of Design Research Ethics*[6] opens with this advice: "If you're feeling uncertain, or nervous, or even just a little weird about something, know that you don't have to handle it on your own. Instead, reach out for support and advice from experienced colleagues, your design research leads, or IDEO's legal counsel." Identify (and continue to refresh) the set of colleagues within or outside your organization who can support you.

---

6 http://lbodre.ideo.com/

The Perils of Fieldwork

Photo by Steve Portigal

R ating/alert systems—in the United States like the much-derided Homeland Security Advisory System or DEFCON (defense readiness condition)—attempt to synthesize enormously complex factors into a linear "amount" of danger. In danger, like in everything else, we harbor a desire for simplistic understandings of complex situations. As long as we remember that reality is more complex and nuanced, these systems are devices for raising awareness and facilitating dialogue.

For research, a peril alerting system might look like this:

1. Social discomfort

2. Physical discomfort

3. Suspicion of hidden danger

4. Fear of visible danger

5. Actual danger

But thanks to the fight-or-flight reflexes that are hardwired into our limbic system and kept away from our consciousness, we can easily conflate these different states (assuming we even have enough information to conclusively assess where we are at). We might feel something like fear—a need to flee—from an awkward conversation. A general feeling of being out of our comfort zone can sometimes escalate from a desire to be elsewhere into an impulse to flee. Culturally, we refer to violent speech or unsafe environments, acknowledging that experiencing emotional harm is different from but as valid as physical harm. But emotional harm—or situations that may lead to emotional harm—may be more of a gray area for researchers. Our brief is to get out of our comfort zone, because that's where we learn the most. Given that, how do we assess the risks we're facing and what do we do about it? What is our obligation to protect ourselves? What should we tolerate?

The stories in this chapter show researchers encountering situations across the range. Jon McNeill finds himself in a socially uncomfortable situation that veers unsteadily into danger. Michael Griffiths, Jen Iudice, and Tom Williams consider how to assess how unsafe things are—and what they can do as a result. Lindsay Moore and Lisa Aronson Fitch are in socially (and sometimes physically) uncomfortable situations. Gavin Johnston reflects on when to give up—or not—in cases of physical discomfort. Jen Van Riet ends up in a socially awkward situation with overtones of danger.

In the 2010 documentary film *Soundtracker*, which profiles nature sound recordist Gordon Hempton, he tells a story about listening for danger, "One particular morning I was in Sri Lanka and knew that I was going to hike up this trail but didn't know exactly where, so in the dark I just kinda put one foot in front of the other and walked into the forest. And there was this beautiful tapestry of insects. I set up my recording gear, but I became overwhelmed with fear. All I knew was something was different, and I felt like I needed to flee, and then I realized, well, this is no fun for me so I'll just let the gear run, and I'll retreat. And then I was listening to it later and enjoying this wonderful composition, and the panic began to return to me. And it was only a few moments after that I could hear the guttural growl of a leopard. And I thought to myself isn't that marvelous. I learned another lesson about what it means to be a listener, and it's to listen to things that are gut level instincts even when you don't have any explanation of it."

While researchers may grow wiser with experience, these stories further illustrate that the very act of stepping out into the "real world" removes control and leaves room for the possibility of peril.

Jon McNeill: Of Speed and Strip Clubs

Relatively early in my career, as I began stepping out and leading studies on my own, I was in Miami Beach doing ethnographic interviews with participatory "drive-alongs" for a luxury car brand. It was the last day in town, and I, with client in tow, had three 3-hour interviews scheduled that had to get done before we could fly out in the morning, the last one being scheduled for 9 p.m. This last interview was with Kenny, a guy who was actually supposed to be interviewed earlier in the week, but had to cancel because his yacht broke down, and he was stranded for the day on a small island off the coast. We hear a lot of different excuses for non-participation, but that was a new one.

My client and I got through our first two interviews that day at around 8, hopped back in the rental car, and started the trip to interview 3, feeling hungry and tired, having missed dinner. I called Kenny to confirm that we were coming, in case he was on another island. He answered in an energetic but distracted tone: "Yeah, laying out the drinks right now. We'll get in the car, go get some speed, and come back and I'll give you whatever you need." Click.

"Speed? Oh no. Who *is* this guy? He must mean going fast in his car," I thought to myself.

I warned my client that we might have a live wire on our hands, but that we'd just go get the interview that we needed and then grab a bite.

We arrived at the address to see Kenny out front, waiting for us. "My wife is putting the kids to bed right now," he told us, "so I'd rather not go in just yet and disturb them. Why don't we get in my car, do the drive, go get a beer, and then come back and do the interview thing?"

We usually did the drive-along as the last part of the interview, but as intrepid researchers, going with the flow is what we do best! Plus, at this point in the day, a drink sounded pretty good. My client and I nodded our agreement and squeezed into Kenny's convertible: me riding shotgun, and my client folded into the tiny backseat area, holding the camcorder.

As soon as I buckled my seatbelt, Kenny hit the gas, and I saw the speedometer jump up to 110 mph. I looked back at my client, white-knuckled, and—like a champ—rolling video on the whole thing.

We rocketed through a number of dark, mostly empty Miami streets. I was disoriented, but loving the way the car gripped the pavement as we took turns in high gear. Just as I was wondering why he was choosing to take us to a bar that was so far from his home, I noticed a police cruiser waiting at a stoplight ahead of us. Either Kenny didn't notice, or he wasn't worried; we flew through the intersection, still doing over 100.

I flashed on how the rest of the evening might unfold: sirens, mug shots, bailing my informant out of jail ... but the cruiser didn't even give chase. I think the officer knew he wouldn't catch us.

Finally, we pulled into a large parking lot, full of expensive cars, in front of a small oblong building. Two huge bouncers stood out front.

Kenny turned to us and said, "Welcome to the best all-black strip club in Miami Beach!" And he headed for the entrance before I could fully process what that meant. My client's mouth was agape.

Neither my client nor I are what you might call "strip club people." He had been telling me about how he and his partner were remodeling their house into a real mid-century modern masterpiece. As I looked down at myself, I saw with dismay that the polo shirt I was wearing kind of made me look like the guy on *Blue's Clues*.

Since this experience, I've heard stories of researchers obliging their clients by taking them to strip clubs, all in the name of client services. And Miami's relationship to strip clubs did seem to be more casual than other parts of the country, because a few of our other participants had mentioned in passing eating lunch or getting a drink at a strip club. But I was mortified—this was not something I was anticipating. Yet, at the same time, I felt cuffed. I knew we had to get this interview checked off, and I didn't feel like I could demand that we return to his home without ruining our chances for building strong rapport.

I turned to my client and said, "I am so sorry. If I had any idea that he was taking us here, I wouldn't have agreed. But at this point, I'm worried about insulting him, so let's just go in, have a quick drink, and head out."

My client, a saint, shrugged and said, "This is just what happens when you do ethnography, right?" Right.

The bouncers patted us down, and we walked inside. Not having any depth of experience in this area, I had to take Kenny's word for it being the best of its kind in Miami. Kenny was already at the bar, waiting with our drinks.

"So, what do you want to know?" he asked me, as he handed me a beer.

I struggled to remember my protocol questions, and we talked for about five minutes before Kenny excused himself to go to the bathroom. I looked over at my client, and we both made a silent acknowledgment that we were done with our beers and ready to go.

Just then, Kenny came back with a stripper on his arm. He turned to my client, "Hey, I bought you a lap dance."

My client's face went white. The room began to spin. My client tried to politely decline.

Kenny, confused, said, "No, she's great, I've had her before!"

My client politely declined again and suggested Kenny go for it.

Kenny asked him, "What is it? Are you married?"

"No."

"You have a girlfriend who would disapprove?"

"No."

"Well, then, what is it?"

My client started stumbling over his words, trying to come up with a firmer excuse. Then Kenny laid down his trump card.

"Look, man, I'm doing this because everyone thinks you're cops. You're white, clearly not having a good time, and if you don't do this, they're probably going to take us outside and beat us up." He waited for my client to answer. My client looked at me the way survivors of a shipwreck must look at the person holding a life preserver. To my shame, I looked away.

My client, resigned, was led back to a private room. I turned back around in my seat and started processing all that had happened: my conversations with my client, some of the things he said that I hadn't caught at the time, his answers to Kenny just then ... and it all suddenly clicked for me, with a sickening certainty.

Kenny handed me another beer and said, "You know, I think your colleague might be gay."

"Yeah," I told him, "I just figured that out myself. But what you don't know is he's actually not my colleague, he's actually my client. You just gave a private lap dance to my gay client."

I felt ill. Kenny started laughing.

"That's really funny, man. That's really funny."

I think Kenny really felt badly about the whole thing. After my client returned, we left, and Kenny took us out to dinner at a kitschy piano bar owned by an old gay friend of his. We all laughed and told stories about crazy things that had happened to us in our lives, and at the end, without us knowing, Kenny paid for everything.

The night ended back at Kenny's house, in front of a literal parking lot full of his Audis, Porsches, and huge SUVs. He was a fantastic informant, and helped me craft the recommendations for the brand based on his interview.

The car ride back to the hotel was pretty quiet. "Strange night, huh?" I said. My client nodded his head.

We shook hands at the hotel elevator and said goodnight. That was the last time I saw him. He wasn't at the final presentation, and I heard that he had left the company not too long afterward.

At the end of the study, we sent him a client satisfaction survey, which was standard practice for us at that time. To my shock, it came back straight 10s. My client was a saint.

This story doesn't paint me in the best light—mistakes were made, character flaws became apparent. But in some ways, the ability to realize that you've made mistakes and are flawed is one of the things I treasure most about anthropology—ever since my Introduction to Anthropology college courses where I began to learn about the long, illustrious line of mistaken and flawed anthropologists who came before me. In fact, often those mistakes and faux pas were the keys to unlocking some heretofore hidden cultural truths. And I think that night was no different, although I don't think the cultural truths that were unlocked for me were necessarily about luxury automobiles.

I can't see myself getting into the same situation now. There were at least two inflection points that night where today I would have directed things differently, but it could be that going through that experience together, the three of us, led to a deeper connection and (eventually) a successful interview. It certainly led to a War Story.

Jen Iudice: Trust Your Gut, It Can Save Your Life!

Having done ethnographic research for nearly 20 years, I've definitely seen it all in the field. Fortunately, that includes coming across some very interesting and enthusiastic participants. On occasion however, there are times when the recruiter misses the boat, things slip through the cracks, and *wham bam*, you are in a painfully uncomfortable or, in rare cases, a dangerous situation. Hence the challenge of screening: striking a balance between actually screening participants while trying not to lead them. As researchers, we are aware of the occasional duds who sneak their way into a study in order to make a buck! This is one of those stories.

Recently, I was charged to do some field research for a client about how people use their personal data—a topic that covered a massive amount of subtopics and could apply to almost anyone. The screener was carefully developed with the client's input, and recruiting provided us with a broad spectrum of participants. Good so far.

The client was very motivated to participate in the research, which is almost always a positive. However, on this particular occasion, my colleague and I were ultimately relieved that he could not make it to this interview!

When we arrived at the location, we noticed an old, rundown, high-rise building with a bail bondsman conveniently located on the bottom floor. There were several "tenants" taking leisurely "naps" in front of the doorway to greet us. At that moment, I felt a terrible sinking feeling in my stomach. My colleague half joking/half seriously said, "I don't want to go in there Jen … I don't care if he uses Mint.com!"

As we drove around the building several times, I contemplated: Am I being too judgmental? Could this really be a well-qualified participant who I am simply not willing to accept because of the sketchy appearance of his place of residence? Can we risk entering this building with all of our expensive electronic/video equipment?

My colleague and I decided not to risk ignoring the feeling in our guts, and we phoned to cancel the interview.

When the participant answered the phone, he sounded very strange and out of sorts. I let him know that we would still pay him for his time, but we could not make it to the interview. (Translation: We are afraid to come into your building!) He then explained that he had just been robbed at gunpoint in his apartment, and that it was a good thing we did not come over! This became even more concerning when we realized that you could not enter this building without going through a security check-in at the front desk. (This was another tip-off that we should not go in!) This event would mean that either the security precautions were a joke, or that someone who lived in the building had robbed him! Needless to say, I did not ask any details, and he continued to talk to me about how distraught he was. I did my best to try and console the man and wished him luck with his situation. AWKWARD!

It boggles my mind to think about what could have happened if we had followed through with this interview! As one could imagine, I "verbalized my concerns" to the recruiter (i.e., I gave them an earful!), but moving forward, I will always map out my in-home interviews and will always make sure that I have a colleague with me on every interview ... just to be safe!

Be careful out there, everyone. Always be aware of your surroundings. If it doesn't feel right, it probably isn't!

Lindsay Moore: Sexism in the City

We were in New York City, on day four of a three-week fieldwork trip. We had had some bumpy interviews the first few days, including a participant who clammed up because her husband was in the room, another who wasn't comfortable showing us any of the software processes she had been recruited to show us, and a third with whom the conversation was like Mr. Toad's Wild Ride, with us hanging on for dear life. But I was finally starting to settle in to the interview guide and was feeling positive about what we were learning. Plus, we were getting a great apartment tour of Manhattan!

We were accompanied on each interview by a rotating member of the client team so that they could all experience the research firsthand, and this day was our first with a particular team member. Our morning interview had gone fairly well, but I could tell our client partner was having some trouble staying in the background, as she was used to more actively managing her interactions with customers.

We walked in the door for our afternoon interview, and I made some small talk, saying something like "How is your day going so far?" to our participant, who was an older gentleman. He answered that it was going much better now that we three pretty girls were there, but that it would be even better if we didn't have clothes on. I experienced a shocked moment of "Did he really just said that???" and took a sidelong glance at my client to see her reaction. She had one of those impenetrable customer service masks of politeness on her face. I tried to shake off the comment and proceeded into the interview.

For the first 30 minutes, I found myself utterly unable to manage the flow with the participant, who would physically turn toward the client to answer my questions, and then turn back to me and say, "You understand?" The interviews were about financial behavior, and he made it very clear that he thought I wouldn't be able to follow what he was saying. Meanwhile, in an effort to be polite, engaged, and responsive with her customer, my client was unintentionally making it worse. I realized I needed to gain some kind of credibility and after the umpteenth "I don't know if you would understand," I told him that I did have some financial background and that I was following just fine. After that, I was much better able to lead the interview, and he engaged directly with me. Still, for another hour and a half, he continued to be condescending and make inappropriate/sexist comments. (The number of times he suggested we "girls" go shopping at Bloomingdale's after the interview? Five. What he wanted us to buy? Blouses.)

After leaving the interview, I was hopping mad and said to my client and my colleague that I couldn't believe what we had just experienced. They agreed but felt like we had still been able to uncover great information in the interview. They also thought that sometimes older men were just "like that" and that I shouldn't let it get to me. I was bothered but decided to let it go. The interview had been uncomfortable but not unsafe, and the client was pleased with what we had learned. As an interviewer, wasn't I supposed to be able to set my own emotions aside?

When revisiting the transcripts and coding the interview data, it really became clear to me that I was not overreacting to what we had experienced. It was blatantly bad. Still, what should we have done? When I've related the story to other friends and colleagues, they've said that we should have left the home after the initial no-clothes comment. I want to agree on principle, but I also know that if I never allow myself to experience something uncomfortable, I'll miss out on the richness and depth that is part of this kind of work. What I do know is that it's okay to share and talk about our own emotional responses to difficult research situations and that doing so is an important part of self-care for researchers. In the future, I will also make sure to have a plan in place with my fieldwork partners for when—and how—to end an interview, so that it's not a process we need to invent in the moment.

Gavin Johnston: It's 4:00 a.m. Do You Know Where Your Ethnographer Is?

The nature of what you're studying and the importance of context is something one should never forget. This is particularly true when the product you're focusing on is a fusion of caffeine-infused malt liquor, Red Bull, and Tang, and it is primarily consumed by hipster 20-somethings as they "pre-funk" on a Friday night. On the surface, it sounds like the kind of thing one hears or reads about and says,

"Oh, poor you," with more than a touch of sarcasm. And to be fair, I'll be the first to admit that doing ethnographic research on a topic like this is decidedly more enjoyable than studying, say, online tax preparation. Or at least it is until it's 4:00 a.m. in the Bronx, the subway has stopped running for the night, and your shoulder is coated in a quickly freezing film of someone else's vomit. This is when knowing your limits and having a back-up plan for getting back to the hotel (or out of jail) becomes as important as the camera, the training, or your research experience.

The fieldwork began with a party being hosted by two young women so obsessed with the drink that they had actually dressed as cans of the product for Halloween. They were experts at finding an amazing number of uses for it, from turning empty cans into art to cooking with the neon liquid. Imagine a float made with a mix of the god-awful stuff and strawberry ice cream. As the party heated up and the list of participants grew, simply keeping up was difficult. Notepads were quickly filling up, and batteries were drained.

Normally, the idea is that you drink one of these concoctions to kick off the evening and one late in the evening, say midnight, to keep the party going. But that wasn't the case with these folks. No, rather than being used to supplement the other drinks throughout the evening, the stuff was consumed exclusively, leading to what they hoped would be "mad adventures" and general mayhem. Being long past my partying days, I took it in stride, assuming it was just bravado. Fieldwork demands vigilance, so if capturing the full context of use meant losing a little sleep and stinking of cigarettes, so be it. But it turned out that much more was required.

At about 1:00, as one of the roommates found a corner in which to sleep away the night, the other grabbed two more cans of the stuff, three of her friends, and me, and then headed for the door, intent on getting to an obscure club in the Bronx. After a walk through a foot or so of snow, we hopped on the subway and headed out of Brooklyn. As it turned out, the obscure club was a warehouse in a deserted neighborhood. At this point, my camera battery had run dry, my notebook was full from cover to cover, and I was running out of steam. As I contemplated calling a cab, I realized that I was too far away, had limited cash, and was in a neighborhood that no cab driver would have driven to in the first place. So I decided to continue on with my participants. In for a penny, as they say.

Not long after, around 3:00, my key informant and one of her friends tracked me down (I had lost them half an hour earlier in the crowd) and asked if I was ready to go because one of their cohorts had consumed "a little too much" booze. We headed for the door. Unfortunately, making it to the subway for the last late-night train was unlikely. Instead, half an hour later, I found myself, my host, and her friends sitting in a subway station that was in disrepair. Thirty minutes after that, sitting on a bench in the frigid subway station, waiting for the 5:00 a.m. train, the friend who had downed a bit too much decided it was a good time to paint my shoulder with the Day-Glo contents of her stomach.

"2 A.M. IN THE SUBWAY ..." (CC BY 2.0) BY WWWARD

The decision to stick with it ultimately resulted in some break-through insights and a very happy client, so I can't complain. But all things being equal, I would do things differently today. The experience helped remind me that it's important to know when to bow out and how you're going to do it. It reminded me that it's important to set limits on what you're willing to do in the name of research, rather than pushing yourself to the breaking point, putting yourself in harm's way, or being party to what may be questionably legal behavior. Of course, six months later I was sitting in a 130-degree attic with HVAC guys for 10 hours at a time. Sometimes, it takes years for these lessons to take hold.

Lisa Aronson Fitch: When Rapport Goes Too Far

While working at a product development consultancy several years ago, I went to Southern California to conduct a series of in-home interviews for a consumer product client. As we all know, it is essential for researchers to develop a rapport with the participants immediately so that they feel comfortable having you in their homes and opening up about their lives, behaviors, and interests. In one particular interview, a degree of rapport, however questionable, developed quickly.

As soon as the door opened, a five-year-old boy appeared in blue footsie pajamas, asking if he could give me and my colleague kisses. My colleague and I exchanged a quick glance because in the car not minutes before, he mentioned that he wasn't very fond of kids. (If I recall, he didn't say it that nicely.) What should we have done? This little boy was waiting with puckered lips. If we had said no or that we were uncomfortable letting him kiss us, we risked alienating the mother who was standing there with a smile; if we said yes, we would have felt uncomfortable knowing this kid was about to do the exact opposite of what a child should do when meeting a stranger. (Didn't this parent ever hear of "stranger danger?") We hadn't even put our bags down yet and introduced ourselves! To make matters worse, as I started to slowly (very slowly) bend down toward the little boy, his mother said, "Remember son, not on the lips!" Needless to say, I was completely confused and disturbed as to why this was all happening. After I received my kiss on the cheek, it was my colleague's turn. The little footsies-clad kid was then sent to bed, and we began the interview with his parents.

While our conversation focused on kitchen routines, my colleague and I struggled with the idea that these parents encouraged their son to kiss strangers. We began to even feel violated as the little boy came running out of his bed six more times through the two-hour interview to give us more kisses. Didn't he care to ask if I was seeing someone at the time? Following the ordeal, I mean interview, my colleague and I discussed the idea of "when rapport goes too far." What should a researcher do in this situation? Should we have accepted kisses from a strange child in the name of developing rapport for a research interview? Should we have suggested to the parents that they teach their child a much different lesson about strangers?

Having grown up around New York City, I'd become properly paranoid about dealing with strangers, so the idea of teaching my child it was all right to kiss strangers made me twitch.

Tom Williams: Go with the Flow

Our ethnography research team visited a small neighborhood health clinic in Beijing to study its workflow. It was 2009 and concern over the H1N1 swine flu was at its peak. There was a special flu screening at the airport, and yet the folks at the clinic seemed concerned that we, as Americans, might be seen as potential carriers of the virus that was causing near panic at the time. To make matters worse, I had awoken that morning with a scratchy throat. It was just a reaction to the hazy air quality in Beijing, but still, it would have been very bad to be coughing in this situation, so in the taxi on the way to the clinic I stuffed multiple cough drops into my mouth.

PHOTO BY TOM WILLIAMS

Doing field research in China is always a little bit surreal for me, as an American. The cultural differences are pretty subtle on paper, but can be stark in person. They reveal themselves in that weird way that cultural differences do: unexpected little variations in design, procedures, or personal manners. In this setting, in particular, lots of little things stood out when first walking into the clinic: the scale to weigh patients was in the waiting area, not near the exam rooms.

Next to the scale was somebody's bicycle, and a broom was propped in the corner. The waiting room chairs were plastic, not upholstered, and there was a vending machine offering free contraception. There were brochures but no magazines.

"How long have you been here in China?" the nurse manager asked us through an interpreter. "Three days," I replied, willing myself not to cough. "Well, we occasionally get unannounced spot-checks by government health officials and, because of the swine flu, if they show up while you're here doing research we'll need you to say you arrived in China two weeks ago, not three days ago."

Huh? What? Lie to Chinese government officials? Is that in my job description? I've seen way too many prison movies to be comfortable with this. Plus, isn't my time in the country a pretty easy thing to check on by just—oh, I don't know—*looking at the stamp in my passport?* And the request was made in such a matter-of-fact, this-is-no-big-deal way that we weren't exactly given a chance to voice our concerns; it was simply on a list of mundane procedures for the day: "The bathrooms are down the hall, you're scheduled to interview two nurses, then two doctors, then you'll do an hour of straight observation, then we're gonna have you lie to government officials, and by then it'll be time for lunch." Ugh! Fidgeting nervously and imagining what would happen if this were a movie, I glanced around to see if there was a back door for a hasty exit. (Of course, fleeing from government officials is surely better than lying to them!)

We were taken to a room for our first interview and the oddness continued: we sat in reclining chairs normally used by dialysis patients. The staff graciously served us tea and watermelon but then placed a bucket in the middle of the floor for seeds and rinds. I was wondering what the bucket was normally used for but decided not to ask. We interviewed a very kind and helpful nurse but she kept a surgical mask on her face the whole time.

But then something happened: it was the simple magic of focusing on what I was there to do—field research. I got absorbed in hearing people tell their stories, obsessing about getting good video and good still photos, asking good questions, and listening closely. I enjoyed the watermelon and stopped worrying about how weird it felt to be spitting watermelon seeds into a bucket during an interview. By letting myself go with the flow, I actually forgot about my scratchy throat and even forgot about the possibility of being confronted about the date I arrived in China.

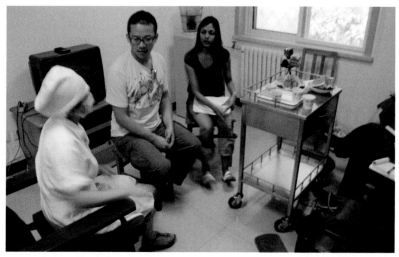

The interviews and observations went very well, and for all my initial impressions of differences, we noticed many similar workflow patterns to clinics that we had studied in the United States and Europe. In the end, there was no surprise visit by health inspectors. After feeling uncomfortable as an outsider at the beginning, by simply sticking to the process and not pushing against prevailing cultural norms, I now felt at ease. We truly bonded with the clinic staff and developed a very solid understanding of their process. We said our good-byes, left the clinic, and walked to a nearby Buddhist vegetarian place for lunch. When we stepped into the crowded restaurant, all the customers turned in unison to look at the foreigners. I reached in my pocket for a cough drop, and the process started all over again.

Jen Van Riet: Jennie's Got a Gun

Long ago, before smartphones were even a blip on the radar, I was the lead researcher on a new text-banking product for feature phones. It was to be one of the very first mobile products developed by my company, and I was super-stoked to be a pioneer in mobile research!

The lead designer and I quickly realized this problem space was more complicated than our newbie minds envisioned. How were we going to design an intuitive product when our North American user base was confused about how text messages even worked? At best, if someone had ever sent a text message, they most likely learned it from televisions shows like *American Idol* (where viewers scrambled to text in support of singers they could not bear to see eliminated).

We devised an approach with a "cheat sheet" that users would keep in their wallets or purses, listing everything they could do with text banking. We wondered how well users would take to the idea of keeping another item in their wallet or purse, so we added questions about this to our research script.

We had a prototype designed and a research protocol developed, but then we struggled to gain access to our end users, as it was a business-to-business product, and we had to work through our customer. After about six weeks of back and forth, red tape, and clearing hurdles, we finally boarded an airplane to Utah to visit a small credit union where we would have access to a handful of our end users. Yippee!

Fresh off the plane, the lead designer and I arrived at the credit union eager to meet our end users one-on-one and get feedback on our ideas. Before we discussed our design ideas, we asked them about what they had in their wallet or purse and if we could see it. This research was a chance to envision how our cheat sheet would co-exist with the other items in people's purses and wallets. Most of the sessions ran smoothly, and in addition to seeing standard items like money and credit cards, we got glimpses of adorable photographs, sentimental notes, and good luck charms.

Toward the end of the day, this big dude—our next participant—walked in. When we asked to see what he carried, he stood up slowly and emptied his pockets on the table. While he did this, I thought how lucky we were that he was willing to reveal so much personal information to us strangers—we sure were learning a lot on this trip! My boss would be proud and our trip would be a success. The contents of his last pocket, however, threw us for a loop when he proudly pulled out a *handgun*! Apparently, it was an important pocket item he wanted to include in the show-and-tell. Perhaps I was sheltered, but I was super uncomfortable for the rest of the interview as I was trying to grasp why he brought a gun to a financial institution and why on earth he decided to pull it out! I was also sure my design partner was going to freak out and leave the room, so I was trying to figure out a graceful way to end the interview early. It turned out this wasn't necessary. My partner surprised me by going off-script and asking the participant a bunch of questions about the gun, including whether she could *hold the gun*! I was completely stunned and felt sheepish for the rest of the interview. We ended up getting rich data in the end, but to this day, I cannot think of a more uncomfortable research session!

Michael B. Griffiths: All About Face (Sichuan Adventures)

I was in Sichuan province, at a small town called Anxian. I was with a U.S. film producer and a Chinese research assistant. We were documenting lower-tier city lifestyles in terms of the human condition, as well as how people consume. We had just finished up our morning session with a man who shared emotional stories about the impact of the 2008 Sichuan earthquake.

We were operating in two groups, doing home visits at different sites. It was time to pick up the other team from the town center and head off to Mianyang, our next destination.

But the other team called in late. There was a problem. The primary informant's mother had returned home and reacted badly to their presence. While we didn't have the details at this point, it seemed that the team could not easily leave the field site. On the phone, I could hear an intense argument in the background.

I had the driver park up around the corner from the site. The junior member of the team came round to meet us, shaking her head and heaving with frustration. Apparently, the situation in the home had turned nasty, and the senior member was trying to deal with it.

The primary informant, aged nineteen, had not told her mother about our research, although she had given us her formal consent. And now her mother was furious with her daughter for not seeking permission, and worse, she suspected us of being cheats or swindlers. We later learned she had been the victim of an identity-theft crime in similar circumstances.

An hour and more passed without a resolution. It seemed ridiculous that we were wasting so much time on this. Could we not just explain the situation, apologize for the inconvenience, and leave? I was inclined to intervene in person, but various team members advised me that a foreigner's presence might exacerbate an already inflammatory situation.

Another phone call came through.

The argument was by now on the street outside the home. The mother was ferociously lashing out and forcibly preventing the senior team member from leaving. Concerned for her safety, I advised that she run around the corner and come over to the car—the site was only 30 meters away.

Once in the car, I proposed that we just leave. We had done nothing wrong, and were increasingly sure this fractious episode was symptomatic of a pre-existing tension between the mother and daughter. Right?

Right! So, let's hit it, driver!

We sped off in the direction of the Mianyang highway.

As we cut through the breeze with the sun in our faces, the team members answered rapid-fire questions and shared their perspectives as they eased themselves out of the tension. We thought we were home free.

Not by a long shot.

Not long had passed before our phones started to ring. Representatives of the local recruitment agency with which we had partnered were with the enraged mother and phoning to ascertain our whereabouts. This was the agency that had recruited the daughter for our research, and I wondered why it seemed beyond their capacity to handle the communication deficit.

We agreed that our overall objectives demanded that we press on with our schedule. Too much time had been wasted, and we were quite clear where we stood in terms of our legal agreement with the informants—the local recruitment agency was better placed and, as we saw it, obligated to resolve any misunderstanding about our identity and purposes.

As a solution, we agreed that the rest of the team would switch off their phones while I would use my phone to call the recruitment agency bosses we dealt with back in Shanghai headquarters. Better to have just one channel of communication open rather than several at the same time.

This we did, but before any intervention could be launched, our driver started to get the same calls from the local recruitment agency. One of our team took the call on the driver's phone and tried to explain our position on the situation and that we just wanted to continue with our schedule. The agency had also helped us plan for further research in Mianyang and Chengdu, so they were well aware of our tight schedule.

If only the situation could have been so simple! Our driver insisted on keeping his phone switched on since this made him available should his employer need to call. Presumably alerted by the local agency representatives, the driver's employer did call and insisted he return to Anxian at once. We were unwilling to return with him since we were unsure whether or not the two-hour return journey would be followed by further time wasted on senseless arguing. Could the situation not be resolved via the proper channels?

Unfortunately, the driver's open line of communication meant that he could be contacted by people other than his boss. He began to get calls from an unfamiliar number over and over again.

Perhaps the driver should switch his phone off, too!?

Then the real shock came.

What? The Public Security Bureau was on the phone? The mother had called the police before we had left. We had left the mother baying for our blood in the street and now the police had arrived to find us gone!

Things went downhill rapidly from there, as arguments erupted about what to do next. Returning to the site would not be an option, the local staff felt, since we would get in trouble for leaving the scene. My explaining things to the local police would not help either, they felt, since the police would not "take my side" because I was a foreigner. Any interaction with the police was bound to be long and protracted anyway, and there was also some notion about market researchers needing to obtain local police permission in advance, which the local recruitment agency had neglected to mention!

Tempers flared, and leadership was called for. But leadership on this project was the same woman who got into the argument with the mother in the first place. She now called her father in a panic!

The idea that the police were actually pursuing us over this appeared ridiculous, but it was very real. We were still driving up the highway away from Anxian, and with visions of flashing blue lights at every intersection, it felt like we were on the run from the law.

It was decision time: the driver had to return to Anxian and could not avoid answering his phone when the police called. We asked him to pull in at a remote roadside restaurant and unload our bags. He would remain with us to get some lunch; it was late afternoon already. Then he would return to Anxian, and his boss would send an alternative driver to take us on to Mianyang.

We ate a meal and for a while believed the heat in the situation had burned itself out. I called in to update our superiors. Apparently, the bosses at the recruitment agency were starting to get a handle on it. There was still disagreement about our next move, but at least the police were not calling us every few minutes. They were probably having lunch, too.

With our phones all back on and the driver gone, the police began calling us directly. Several hours had passed since the original incident, and the mother's demands had become more specific: she wanted the tapes we had recorded in her home. This presented a problem for our research, and our film producer was particularly against this: his movie would be incomplete without these tapes. Moreover, even if we returned the tapes to the mother, the professional format meant she wouldn't be able to play them.

Our conversations thus became more practical and technical as the police sought to broker a mutually satisfactory solution to the problem. An agreement was struck whereby the majority of the team would proceed to Mianyang while two personnel would return to Anxian with the tapes and play these for the mother at the local police station.

It was well into the evening when we arrived in Mianyang, about the same time as our team representatives arrived back in Anxian. After a torrid day, they had to sit and play through the entire four hours of footage for the purposes of the mother's verification. With the police there with her, she gradually adjusted herself to the idea that we were not crooks or foreign spies and found a way to climb down from her rage while saving face.

Exhausted, we spared a thought for the daughter who was probably going to get the raw end of whatever remaining anger could not now be justifiably directed anywhere else. Our analysis of the film footage revealed a wealth of insights into a specific tension between the daughter's almost angelic nature and her mother's oppressive, almost ogre-ish nature. It appeared our fieldwork had exposed an underlying tension after all.

Takeaways

- **Don't go into the field alone.** Two people are usually safer than one. And having a partner to help you assess the situation will help you make good decisions. Establish a code word or phrase to signal each other to end the interview in case of a safety issue.

- **Before you go into the field, know your limits and those of your colleagues.** Those limits may be different.

- **Use the buddy system.** Let someone know where you are going, whom you are meeting with, and when you are planning to be done. After you wrap up the interview, send them a text message.

- **Look before you go.** Tools like Google Street View can give you a visual of your destination—and the neighborhood.

- **Consider the difference between uncomfortable and unsafe.** Are the signifiers of low income (which in the West might be derelict cars and unmaintained property) signifiers of danger or just different environmental norms?

- **Be mindful of what you take into the field and how you display it.** Mobile phones, video cameras, prototypes, and incentives are all potential targets for acquisition.

- **Keep in mind that the interview is a fixed duration.** An uncomfortable situation will be over and done within a couple of hours. If it doesn't hurt, can you put up with it?

- **Practice your observer's distance.** When behavior or circumstances make you uncomfortable, make a note of your own reaction and consider that data.

- **You are a participant in this research, not an observer.** If the respondent is causing your unsafe feelings, you may want to ask them to stop the unsafe behavior. This could be appropriate if the behavior is "waving a gun around," but probably not for "generally being scary."

- **Make sure to debrief with your teammates about their feelings of discomfort, fear, and danger.** It's crucial to process the experience, so you can understand and accept the different perceptions you may have each had and to help clarify the differences between those feelings.

CHAPTER 9

People Taking Care of People

Photo by Steve Portigal

W e use the term *participant observation* to describe a key attribute of user research: you observe by participating. In anthropology, with its legacy of lengthy, immersive fieldwork, the way the one informs the other is obvious. But in applied user research, we often work in a more transactional fashion, functionally and therefore emotionally. We screen individual participants based on preselected criteria, we schedule interviews to begin and end at certain times, and we provide a monetary incentive at the conclusion of the interview. The context in which we work formalizes the divide between "researcher" and "participant."

Of course, the work is intensely and expressly about people and infused with concern for people. Open-ended interviews that emphasize listening and following up are compassionate at their core. We strive to avoid presumptive questions (as in the traditional "How long have you been beating your wife?") not only because they are unreliable, but also because they are unkind.

Having participants sign an informed consent document is more about providing legal protection for the researcher and her sponsors than it is about protecting the participant, but its origins are ethical—to ensure that we don't repeat the horrific abuses of the not-so-distant past.[1]

And presumably the whole reason we are in the field to begin with is because we hope after the research is complete to make some aspect of life better for some people. Sometimes we strive to make things better in the moment, before we conclude the transaction. After an interview about a bank account, where the participant began to cry in frustration, my client made it clear to our participant how she should seek to resolve the underlying issues, with specific information about my client's plans to follow up. In another study, I interviewed a young man who owned a house, was married with two small children and another one due imminently, was active in his church and with his extended family and his work, but was clearly wired so that he needed some work-arounds to complete ordinary tasks (such as ordering his closet by ROYGBIV[2] and scheduling reminders at work to ensure that he would get up to use the bathroom). At the conclusion of the interview, after we declined to join them for dinner, my client very kindly recommended that this young man look into

---

1 Such as the Tuskegee Syphilis Experiment, a clinical study conducted by the U.S. government from the 1930s through the 1970s: http://rfld.me/tuskg

2 http://rfld.me/ROYgBIV

Mindfulness-Based Stress Reduction. In both cases, we used the framework of the transaction to guide us in our decisions about when—and how—to intervene.

In a contrasting experience, I interviewed a mother about food preparation. We went deep into the personal aspects of food and home. We talked about the gastric bypass operations that she and her daughter had gone through together. She spoke bitterly about her own childhood and the lack of nurturing—whether through food or any other form—from her own mother. We covered what we needed to cover in an appropriately discursive fashion, and as we were heading toward the natural (and scheduled) conclusion of the interview, something changed abruptly. This woman clearly was deeply in need of support, and in a moment, the dynamic in the interview began to shift so that her primary objective was to talk about her own unresolved issues. This shift was dramatic, obvious, and felt "wrong." I was neither obligated nor qualified to provide counseling and having felt the interview turn a corner into something else, I concluded it, and we made our exit more rapidly than I have ever done before or since. This woman and I had different boundaries and to protect both of us, I stopped the interview.

But this is ambiguous terrain. There's an unspoken ideal that we aim for, keeping things "pure," maintaining a neutral stance where we neither judge nor harm but also don't aid. When we watch someone struggle to use our product, we're right in the midst of this. In *The Vulnerable Observer* (subtitled *Anthropology That Breaks Your Heart*), Ruth Behar delves into the challenges the researcher faces, "Even saying '... this is fieldwork,' is ... a method to drain anxiety from situations in which we feel ... helpless to release another from suffering, or at a loss as to whether to act or observe."

In "Friends First. Then Design."[3] John Collery articulates the necessary challenge of creating real human connections with the people we design for. I disagree with how he frames this connection as *friendship*. The interesting territory for us to navigate as researchers is the unmapped space between transient and persistent relationships, between transactions with strangers and connections with friends.

In the stories that follow, circumstances both unusual and prosaic open up opportunities to connect beyond what the research "transaction" presupposes. Although the sources of the messes vary, Sharon

---

3 http://rfld.me/DsgnFr

Cartwright and Nancy Frishberg each help participants clean up. Ilona Posner deals with a bleeding participant. Dan Soltzberg, experiencing discomfort himself, changes his own behavior to prevent discomfort in another. Rachel Shadoan and her colleague are forced into alternate and less-effective ways of self-care in the field. Fumiko Ichikawa deals with the breakdown of an individual on the project team, and does her best to help take care of her. Apala Lahira Chavan witnesses a household situation collapse and is stymied as to how to respond. The empathy these researchers display is at the core of why they are doing research in the first place and also is at the core of what makes for good research.

Sharon Cartwright: Broken Windows Theory

We were surprised that Anna wasn't at home when we arrived at her house. We could see through the lounge windows that the house was empty of furniture and personal belongings, adding further to the intrigue. We had followed our usual protocol of sending an email confirmation clearly stating the time of the research session, and Anna had been called the day before to confirm.

We decided to try calling Anna. She picked up our call as she was coming up her driveway. She was running late and seemed a bit agitated, telling us that she had locked herself out an hour earlier. She was just moving into this house and didn't have a spare key yet. She'd decided, in the interest of proceeding, that she was going to smash a window to get in and had just called around to her brother's house to pick up the appropriate tools.

Anna seemed like a practical woman, and smashing her front door window didn't seem to daunt her. I indicated that there was no need to take such drastic action for our sakes. But she was adamant and was soon taking a hammer to the glass panel in the kitchen door.

Once inside, Anna, the client (who'd come along for the ride), and I began the clean-up. I manned the vacuum cleaner and mused over the start to the session. There was something bonding about a shared clean-up!

We were there to observe Anna set up wireless broadband. On a good day, the process wasn't straightforward; we had already seen several participants struggle through it. Over the next two hours, we observed Anna encountering several technical issues with hardware and software. She managed to resolve some issues on her own. Many times, she resorted to calling the contact center, although their advice was mixed—sometimes helping Anna, sometimes complicating matters.

We had scheduled the session for 1.5 hours, expecting this to be sufficient, but many sessions—including Anna's—extended over this. After two hours, Anna had not succeeded in setting up her wireless broadband connection. Unable to stay any longer, we were disappointed to leave without seeing Anna ultimately succeed. We wished her luck, because she was clearly going to need it.

During the two hours we spent with her, Anna revealed a few things to us. Her long-term relationship had recently ended, explaining her move to Auckland. She was also looking for work. Her ex-partner's teenage son had generally taken the lead on the technology front in their home, and it was dawning on her that this was now her role.

With the significant life stresses she was facing, it was hard to watch her struggle through a technology setup that should have been easier, dare I say "simple." While we learned that setting up a wireless Internet often happens during a time of stress, since it's one task of many when you move, I felt for Anna and the difficult time she was going through.

Nancy Frishberg: Look Sharp

I worked on a project that involved people who had a chronic illness. This project had me meeting with a half dozen people individually in their homes or workplaces three times over a two-month period, and accompanying each of them to the specialist's office once during that time. In the interviews, our questions ranged from how long they had been living with this condition to how it was diagnosed to how their illness did or didn't limit them.

Meeting people in their homes is sensitive. On the one hand, you're a guest, and on the other, you're there for business. Do you accept a soft drink or take your own? Do you take a snack to share or something for the kids, or does that make it too personal? How soon do you all feel confident that the recording device is no more intrusive than a pencil?

The youngest person in the study just fit into our age limits (35–65 years). A schoolteacher, she knew the most direct and least trafficked drive to the high school. Her son was almost grown, and he spent part of his time at his dad's house, so she was on her own a lot. The first time I called on her it was nearly Christmas time.

She was open and easy about her illness with me, about her grandfather who also had the same condition, and about her dad who had become a pharmacist in order to be better equipped to help people with chronic illnesses. She invited me into her bathroom to see the array of medications she kept handy, and into her kitchen where she stored the syringes and medication in the fridge. That's when I noticed five sharps collectors on top of the refrigerator—those red plastic translucent boxes you've seen at the doctor's office that hold used syringes or other medical waste. In the U.S., red is the color of danger, and these boxes have an additional red label with the words "warning" and "biohazard," plus more small print. I took a photo or two, and we continued our conversation.

She asked if I would help her set up the artificial Christmas tree, since she was uncertain if she'd be able to do it on her own. I—a nice Jewish girl—had never assembled an artificial Christmas tree, but I figured I could help her if it just involved steadying the parts while one of us inserted the trunk-bits into each other. She was very appreciative when we finished. I was thinking, this is a little boundary violation between my stance as an outsider—interviewer—and her willingness to treat me as an insider—friendly visitor, not terrible, and not worth making a fuss about it, as we're developing this great rapport.

On a subsequent visit a few weeks later, we wandered into the garage. Maybe she was taking out the trash, and I was following her. Or maybe I had parked behind the house that time, and she was letting me out the back way. That's when I saw a dozen more red sharps collectors on the table in the garage. I had to ask, as I snapped a photo, "So where do you dispose of the sharps?" She responded that it was difficult for her to find a time since she commuted to work, and the hospital's office that handled this was closed over the weekend (or was it? she wasn't certain), and it had been many months. Maybe never, since she started on this drug regimen. OK, so duly noted. But it bothered her, and she wanted to be rid of them. Now there were so many, she just was embarrassed to take them all at once. It had become a problem.

On my last home visit, we caught up on all the regular questions and those that were reserved for this final visit. Then she asked me if I would dispose of the sharps containers for her. I said no, but that I would drive her to the hospital, which was nearby, in the same complex as her doctor's office, and we could do it together.

I'm not sure I ever fully articulated the reason I said "No, but ..." (to myself or to her). In a previous life, I was a sign language interpreter, where we had a very clear code of ethics. (For example, what's interpreting vs. what's acting on behalf of the client, when is speech protected, and so on.) By "very clear," I mean it's written down, and the test for becoming an interpreter challenges the candidate's ability to make decisions and justify them. From working with disabled people, I learned that there are many forces that make it easy to create dependency. I'd prefer to reduce dependency: let everyone ask for the specific help they want or need, rather than providing it without asking. In the role of a "business ethnographer," or whatever we call ourselves this week, it seemed like cleaning up the subject's trash was not a task to be outsourced to the ethnographer. Had I said "yes," it would have muddled her perception of my role.

We loaded my rental car with as many red boxes as we could find and drove just a short distance over to the hospital. Sure, we got a few raised eyebrows in the pharmacy as we came in, loaded down with red sharps containers, but she breathed a sigh of relief as I dropped her at home. This act definitely felt like we had crossed some boundary, and yet, I didn't want to be an automaton. She had been living with this visible evidence of her own difficulty in confronting a task related to her illness. It was just a few minutes of my time, and a big weight lifted from her.

I think of her and the others in that cohort from time to time, and wonder how they are coping with their illness, now nearly 10 years later. As there is no cure, I'm hopeful they're each managing their condition well. And, I'm hopeful (though not confident) that following that clean-up together, it might have been easier for her to take just one or two red boxes to the hospital pharmacy on her own.

Ilona Posner[4]: First Stop the Bleeding!

Around the year 2000, homes with Internet service were rare. AOL was plastering the planet with CDs that promised free Internet. Modems were uncommon and expensive. Online access usually required a modem card installed inside a computer case by a service technician, at a significant cost. My client, the largest Internet Service Provider in Canada, was redesigning its self-installation package for its DSL service; today this would be called a DIY kit.

The goal of our research project was to evaluate the customer experience. It entailed contacting customers who had just ordered the package, interviewing them about their order experience, and asking to visit their homes to observe the installation of the hardware and setting up the service. We visited many homes and observed people with diverse technical experience trying to install this package. The success rate of the customers completing this self-installation within our allotted two hours was very low. We had to suffer silently watching their ordeals: searching among numerous papers and user manuals that accompanied the package for the correct documents and locating the required identification codes; mixing up phone and Internet cables; moving their furniture so that the provided cables

---

4 This author, with a lifetime of experiencing confusion over the capital "I" and lowercase "l" in her first name, asked to be credited with all caps (ILONA POSNER) to eliminate ambiguity. Although her name appears in this book using traditional capitalization, this footnote serves to clarify the correct spelling of her name.

would reach their destinations; and trying to explain their problems in repeated phone calls with technical support.

In some cases, after observing them struggle for two hours and realizing they were incapable of completing this task unaided, we felt so sorry for them that before departing, we completed the installation process on their behalf. We felt bad that they would have to spend additional days waiting, making additional phone calls to arrange for a technician's visit, and dealing with the additional costs of assisted installation. That way, we also were able to witness their excitement and gratification of getting online; for some, it was their first time.

"ANTEC P150 SIDE OPEN FROM REAR" (CC BY 2.0) BY MIKE BABCOCK

I clearly remember one participant who actually was able to successfully complete the installation, and it "only" took him 1.5 hours to do it. He was a male in his early 30s, and a technical writer by profession. His PC had 32MB of RAM, and was running Windows 95.

He already had a modem, but was switching to this new high speed service. He had to remove the internal ISA modem card from his PC tower in order to install the provided Ethernet card. He was more confident and comfortable at this task than most of our other participants. While our camera rolled, he confidently skimmed documents and manuals, even when they were different manuals from the devices that he was dealing with at the time. He opened his PC without difficulty. He proceeded to remove the internal modem card from deep inside his PC case. In the process, he cut his hand on one of the sharp internal edges of the metal case. His hand started to bleed! Blood got on his hardware. We had to interrupt our observations to assist him in stopping the bleeding.

After completing our research, we redesigned the package. We reduced the number of documents and numbered each one for easy reference. (Unfortunately, this simple and usable solution only lasted until the next rebranding exercise conducted by the marketing department, who did not inherit our design rationale.) We rewrote the instructions, using beautiful visuals. We also included a special highlighted warning, "Please be careful when opening your computer case, there are many sharp edges inside."

I wonder if anyone ever noticed that warning message.

Dan Soltzberg: Focus, No Matter What!

I was doing fieldwork for a project on at-home computer use, and a client and I were at "Richie's" house—a double-wide in a Mid-Peninsula mobile home park. Richie's small-to-begin-with mobile home was filled with heavy wooden furniture, boxes of paperwork, and old pieces of technology, making it feel even smaller. We were sitting at the kitchen table, and Richie was saying that he liked to lie on the couch and work on his laptop, so I asked him if we could go into the living room so he could show us.

We re-situated in the living room, and when Richie started opening up emotionally about how meaningful his work was to him, I got down on one knee next to the couch so that I would be on eye level with him, rather than standing over him. As Richie was talking, I was totally focused on listening to him and guiding the conversation forward, but in the back of my mind—somewhere really far in the background—I was aware of a strange cold feeling in my leg.

In addition to leading the interview, I was also manning the video camera and shooting stills, so I wasn't able to give this strange feeling much bandwidth. When we finished our conversation and I stood up, I saw that there was a wet spot on my khaki pants. A wet spot that covered the area from the middle of my shin to above my knee. A massive wet spot.

I hadn't figured out yet what it was, but I knew I'd kneeled in something liquid that was lurking in Richie's carpet. One of the cardinal rules is, I don't make research participants feel bad, and I figured if Richie saw that this had happened, he would only feel bad. So I followed him back into the kitchen, conducted the rest of the interview, paid and thanked him, and left, all the while keeping my wet-spotted leg as much out of Richie's sight line as possible. As far as I know, he had no idea I'd been befouled.

The day's next interview was scheduled tightly, and there was little time to take stock of things. I thought about doing a quick pant leg wash in a gas station bathroom, but made a judgment call that showing up at the second interview with a soaking wet pant leg would be worse than whatever was already starting to dry, so I decided to let it be. As I drove, my leg continued to dry, and it became apparent from the emerging smell that the mystery liquid was cat pee.

The 10-inch wet spot dried to a hard, shiny, stinky consistency as I pulled up to our next interview. The woman we were interviewing had a house that was neat as a pin, and let's just say that she was not an easygoing type of person. I sat as far across the living room as I could, but I could only imagine during the whole interview that she could smell my ripening leg. Let's hope not. Nothing to do but keep calm and carry on.

Rachel Shadoan: Research, in Sickness and in Health

It was my first field assignment out of school. OK, technically it wasn't my assignment—a contractor would be conducting the interviews, and I would be along to observe and record. But I'd spent the previous two years and six months in a lab writing code, so I would take what I could get. To say that I was excited would be an understatement. I was stoked.

Plus, I'd get to fly to California! I'd be on an honest-to-goodness business trip! It was going to be great.

It certainly started out great. In the shuttle from the airport to the hotel, I counted citrus trees. Citrus trees! Growing in the ground! In people's yards! And no one seemed shocked by this! Of course, I had plenty of time to count those trees, as we crawled through traffic for hours. But the weather was glorious, and I, like it, was ebullient.

Things began to look dicey, however, when I met the researcher I would be working with. She was a smart, gregarious woman, who also happened to be sick. Very sick. Down-a-bottle-of-Nyquil-and-sleep-it-off-for-a-week sick.

Rest and recuperation, unfortunately, were luxuries we could not afford. The project was on a tight timeline and already behind. At least one of the interviews we had planned had been rescheduled once. Stakeholders across three organizations were chomping at the bit. It was, in the melodramatic way of business schedules, do or die.

And so we did. We pre-gamed with Thai food, guzzling tom yum soup for its sinus-clearing properties before returning to the hotel for an early-to-bed night. The following morning we set off—my compatriot fueled by a powerful cocktail of cold medicine and espresso, myself running mostly on nerves and the delicious feeling of being free of my cubicle confines.

Still, we felt uncomfortable taking sickness into the homes of our participants. "Give us your insight, and we'll give you the plague!" is not the most enticing slogan a researcher could come up with. We tried to minimize risks. I shook hands with the participants; she abstained. She positioned herself as far away from them as their living rooms and rapport-building would allow, with me, a human note-taking buffer, in between. We strove not to be vectors of disease.

Given the circumstances, the first two interviews went well. But after hours of driving hither and yon across the north Bay Area, in traffic that I would have avoided navigating even with a clear head, my partner's energy began flagging and the cold medicine was wearing off. She tossed back an emergency booster of DayQuil in a Starbucks parking lot, and we steeled ourselves for the final interview. It was perhaps more disorganized than the first two interviews, but we muddled through together.

And then, as the sun sank below the side of the endless freeway, it was over, and we were once again untroubled by the inflexibility of a corporate system that put us in the ethical quandary of whether to conduct fieldwork—or work at all—while ill. We parted ways at a BART station. She headed home to collapse into a restorative, cold-medicine-induced coma; I went into the city to spend a few days basking in the glow of more-or-less-successful fieldwork.

My basking didn't last long, of course. In no time at all, I had a cold.

Fumiko Ichikawa: Good-bye, Cruel World

In May 2008, I coordinated what I call an *inspiration study* concerning healthy eating. What do Japanese people eat and drink? Why? Is there a particular tradition or habit that people have developed around eating? How are the perceptions of eating and health related in Japanese culture? My mission was to make sure that my client's researchers had all the exposure they could imagine around how Japanese people buy, cook, and eat, through interviews, observations, and my own experiences.

One day, our interview took place in the residential area of East Kanagawa, an hour-and-a-half from Tokyo. Our informant was a housewife in her late 40s. She expressed a clear preference about her choice of vegetables, for the sake of the well-being of her husband and two children. She offered us pickled vegetables and soft bamboo shoots, all homemade and requiring time and dedication to prepare. She also allowed us to see what was inside her refrigerator, which some would consider a brave act, as many housewives whom I met considered this area to be far more private than their bedroom or toilet!

The interview went fairly well. She was very relaxed and open, and I felt that we got more than we came for. But there was one minor glitch: the interpreter we hired was not quite the person we hoped her to be.

The interpreter came from an agency, arranged by my fellow researcher. An hour before the interview, she appeared at the meeting point, and we had a chat. She was a lady in her late 30s with a soft, elegant smile. Dressed in a white jacket with a stitched camellia flower, she appeared to me to be very sophisticated. The way she spoke to us prior to the interview was soft but confident, and until the actual interview started, I had no doubts.

As the interview progressed, I noticed that my clients appeared confused. The interpretation concentrated on facts and did not convey the emotion and the passion that we were clearly seeing from the housewife, with her big smiles and gestures. Thirty minutes passed by and after some struggle, my client asked in a very polite way that the interpreter stop. From that point on, the client asked the questions, and I became the interpreter. This change of setup was done quite discreetly, and I do not think that the housewife noticed much.

Dismissing someone on the spot was not an easy thing. It was awkward and challenging. But I felt my client addressed the matter in a very professional way. After we left the informant's home, I saw that my client stepped away from the rest of the group and approached the interpreter, to talk with her about why she had done that. From a distance, the interpreter appeared calm. I assumed that despite the situation, she took things well.

Soon after this interview, the study was complete, and my clients went back to the States. But four days later, in the middle of the night, I received an international call: it was my client. I called her back. She told me that she had received an email from that interpreter, and

I should read this as soon as possible. In the email, the interpreter had written eloquently about how humiliated she was on that day. This email was in fact a suicide note, telling us "I have no choice but to kill myself."

I felt like someone had hit my head real hard. There was a tremendous rush of anxiety, anger, and confusion. How could this happen? What did we do wrong? Why was she reacting this way? Despite the odd hours, we frantically called her and her agency. After three or four hours, we confirmed there was nothing wrong with her. We learned it was simply her way of expressing her anger and making sure we felt sorry for her.

"Lip! Lip my stockings!" a Japanese call girl shouts in the film *Lost in Translation*, as she forces the American celebrity actor played by Bill Murray to "rip" her stockings in his hotel room. The combination of exposure to foreign culture and the wrong interpretation can generate confusion, frustration, and oftentimes, laughter. But on that day, it was mostly confusion that the experience brought me. Sometimes, we experience foreignness in our own culture.

Apala Lahiri Chavan: Whose Side Is the Researcher On?

In one of the very early research projects I worked on in India, we learned many best practices that became part of our research guidelines. However, there were parts of the experience that I have not quite gotten over, even after 12 years.

We were researching in-home media usage in India for a multinational tech company from the U.S. The research targeted lower middle-class households from across the country, both urban and rural. My colleague Amita and I were covering the northern Indian state of Punjab. This particular evening, we were visiting a semi-urban household near the city of Chandigarh.

It was 6 p.m. when we reached the location. We had to leave the car behind and walk the last few yards since the lane was too narrow. As we entered the gate of the house, a group of ladies came out of the house and welcomed us. They had marigold garlands for us to wear and a lit earthen lamp with which to ward off evil spirits.

We were welcomed inside the house and ushered into a tiny but neat living room. One elderly lady who had garlanded us was the mother-in-law. She invited us to sit on a rug on the floor. She sat down too and so did a number of other people—the entire neighborhood was there.

The mother-in-law and some of the other elderly women from the neighborhood did their own in-depth interview where we were the participants! We were asked about our age, income, husbands, caste, education, number of children, size of house, TV serials we watched, and so on. On hearing that neither of us had children although we were married, a hush descended upon the group. After a few tense moments, the mother-in-law told us to have faith in God and not give up hope. We looked down into our plates, wondering what would happen if we told them that we did not have children out of choice!

Some young girls had also joined the gathering inside the living room (which had spilled out to the gate and into the kitchen). One girl rushed home to get us some dessert that she had made that day!

By the time the *gup-shup* (friendly chatter) was over, it was 7:30 p.m. Even though we were used to the fact that time stretched quite a bit in India and hence a session slated for an hour could stretch to an hour and a half (after all, the concept of time in India was circular unlike the linear concept of time in the West), this was beyond what either of us had experienced. But there was no possibility of hurrying anybody. How could we tell a group of extremely hospitable and warm people that our time was more important than their company?

At last, we started the session with the mother-in-law and daughter-in-law. As we realized that the neighbors were not about to leave, Amita and I looked at each other and decided that it was fine to have the neighbors present since they were clearly like a large, extended family.

As the father-in-law, two sons, and the other daughter-in-law were not back from work yet, this was women's time. However, it became clear within the first ten minutes that this daughter-in-law was not going to speak her mind in front of her mother-in-law and the other neighborhood matrons. We did some quick improvisation: I asked the daughter-in-law to show me the house (they knew this would be part of the interview) while my colleague continued to speak with the mother-in-law. This worked very well and while she showed me the house I got to hear the daughter-in-law's story (e.g., how she never got to watch any television she wanted or listen to any music she chose, and so on).

It was 8:30 p.m. or so when the men of the house returned from work. Instantly, the atmosphere changed. Until then, the mother-in-law and the other matrons had been the "bosses" of the session, but now everything changed. The father-in-law and the two sons were clearly in control. The mother-in-law now scurried about between the kitchen and living room and many of the neighborhood matrons and girls left. This was a very high power distance culture[5] after all!

We were fortunate that we had the time to speak with the ladies while the men were not around. Had they been around from the beginning, we would not have heard any of the ladies speak. Even as we carried on the conversation with the men, we suddenly noticed that there was a young lady standing at the living room door. There was a hint of aggression in her posture that made it difficult to ignore her. However, everyone else in the room seemed to not even see her.

Then, as the elder son was telling us about his media usage preferences, a most unexpected thing happened. The young lady at the door suddenly stormed into the room and started addressing us.

---

5 http://rfld.me/CultPwr

She screamed and howled about the physical abuse and dowry harassment[6] she was being subjected to by her husband (the son who was speaking) and the mother-in-law. She shouted, "He made my poor parents buy him that expensive TV that he has been talking about. Now he wants them to buy him a VCR. Where are they going to get the money for that?"

We were absolutely stunned and just as we began to get our wits together, her husband got up, caught her by the hair, and gave her two resounding slaps across the face. He told her—in the most abusive language—to go up to her room.

Enough was enough. Both of us sprang up to our feet and stood between the man and his wife. He was unperturbed and tried to pick up the thread of the conversation with us, as if nothing had happened. His parents said, "This daughter-in-law is a bad woman and needs to be kept in control since she shames us."

We were still standing in front of the daughter-in-law who was now alternating between weeping bitterly and screaming in rage. We had to make a critical decision. What should we do? What was our role in this situation? We were researchers who were supposed to maintain our neutrality and objectivity, but was that the right thing to do? Should we not call the police's Crimes Against Women section and complain about the husband and his parents? Should we not protect this woman who was being abused?

But before we could do anything, the daughter-in-law ran out of the house screaming and made a dash for the main gate. Not one of her family responded, and they told us to ignore the *nautanki* (drama) and continue the conversation.

We said to the family that we would not be able to continue, given what had happened. We handed over the cash incentive and walked out of the house. We looked up and down the lane, but we could not see the daughter-in-law anywhere. It was a little after 10 p.m. when we got into our car and drove off.

I have not been able to come to terms with that one incident, even today. I felt that in order to be a "good" researcher I had betrayed that girl who was being abused and a much larger cause. Should one not be an activist ethnographer, when the situation demands?

---

6 An attempt to obtain more money or goods from a wife's family after the marriage: http://rfld.me/DHrss

Takeaways

- **You can't fix everything.** The more time you spend with people learning about their lives, the more problems you will uncover. It's not possible to fix them all. When you end your interview, those problems will still be present. Consider that your interest and compassion may provide comfort for the moment.

- **Remember that this is ambiguous territory.** You may feel the pull to connect, you may be conflicted about how much connection is feasible or appropriate, and you may be dissatisfied when you depart.

- **Consider if and when to connect beyond the interview.** If you are moved to go beyond the perceived transactional relationship, consider whether to do so before, during, or after, not only in terms of your research objectives, but also when it may be most comfortable for the participant.

- **Compassion can be invisible and visible.** Consider both invisible compassion (the feelings you cultivate toward another person) and visible small kindnesses (the action you take toward that person) as different approaches that can each have a profound impact. Choosing to be compassionate may be an easier first step, and this will ultimately direct your actions.

- **Keep the transaction in mind.** Regardless of what else you observe that moves you, your participant has agreed to speak with you based on expectations that you set. You can respect them by (mostly, or entirely) sticking with the plan.

- **Consider that it's within your power to choose to walk away.** Not everyone shares the same sense of boundaries. You can fall back on the transaction to protect yourself and them. As I've said before, knowing when to walk away is something we develop over the course of our lives.

- **The moments in the field that take us off-script highlight a gap between your assumptions and your participant's mental model.** That deviation can reveal a deeper insight.

CHAPTER 10

Can't Stop the Feeling

Photo by Steve Portigal

I hope to see a participant cry in every study I'm involved in. This isn't about my heartless desire to *make* people cry. I'm not talking about forcing people to suffer through a terrible user experience until they burst into tears of frustration. I'm looking for those moments of intense rapport, where what the participant shares with me is so real that their emotions come to the surface.

Perhaps some of this is just my own ego gratification, because I believe that if we do this work well, just about any topic can connect to people's deeper (often, but not always sad) emotions. I was doing research about the design of wine labels, and a woman began to cry quietly during our interview, explaining that the small footprint on the Barefoot Wine label reminded her of her struggles to conceive a child. Of course, I felt compassion for her struggle, but I was touched that she felt safe enough to share something so personal that went miles beyond "I like the blue one." I wasn't seeking her tears specifically, but I always strive for honest sharing without regard to my agenda. Then it's up to me what I do with that.

In a different study, a young woman shared many stories about her personal background, choices, and life goals. She articulated a philosophy of leaning into uncertainty and its associated freedom, rather than being constricted by more traditional paths. As the conversation continued into its second hour, I suddenly realized that the entire time she'd been sitting beneath a large piece of art that showed a rope bridge enshrouded in mist leading into the murk toward a heavily concealed land mass. I had been so transfixed by her story that I hadn't realized that she was sitting beneath a visual representation of her themes. Or so it felt to me. I decided to shift the interview to the bigger picture (so to speak), asking "This may seem like a *non sequitur*, but it's not—can you tell me about that artwork?" She began to cry as she explained the picture's symbolism and how she acquired it, and then revealed her deeper insecurity about the unclear path she was on. Again, I wasn't pleased by her distress, but I was pleased that my interest helped her feel safe in sharing. Indeed, she became increasingly animated, and as we later began to wrap up the interview, it was clear that she would be quite happy to have us stay and continue to talk. The next day she sent me a thank you email! I don't believe asking the question that led her to tears was hurtful. The opportunity I created was beneficial to her. It was also beneficial to our research objective, where we were seeking a deeper understanding of the factors that inform people's choices.

In addition to the emotions exhibited by our participants, we also must deal with the emotions we experience, although whether we choose to express them or not is of crucial importance. Early in my career, my colleague Tom Williams (see his story "Go with the Flow" in Chapter 8, "The Perils of Fieldwork") and I met with a young mother, overflowing with positive energy, who revealed at the beginning of the interview that she was fighting cancer. The interview itself was about drinking water, and her cancer was relevant in that she had incorporated water into her practice for visualizing improved health. When she straightforwardly told us about having cancer, we mirrored her matter-of-fact tone and reacted very little. Importantly, we did not do what most of us would do in a social setting—make that backward hiss, the sharp intake of breath, followed by "Oh! I'm so sorry!" Our facial expressions and body language were neutral—not disinterested, but neutral. We remained fully engaged, listening raptly. We asked questions about her treatment, in terms of how she incorporated drinking water. We did not shy away from the facts. But we considered both her tone and our role and did not act on our discomfort, fear, or sadness. I remember very precisely the feeling inside that I held onto, a sense of wanting to scream and weep. And while I wouldn't do that, the social norm of "I'm so sorry" is in many cases more about us than the other person. We say "sorry" because we don't know what else to say and that small action makes us feel a bit better. But the role of interviewers empowered us to put the emotions of the other person ahead of ours. My emotions were running very high, but I kept them to myself. Tom and I waited until we left the interview to deal with our emotions. But not in the interview. That was her time.

NOTE MAKE TIME FOR SELF-CARE

I was a participant in a design sprint-style workshop focused on ways to help people with cancer. When we arrived for the workshop, we were told we would be building prototypes and then presenting them to cancer patients and survivors. Within the design sprint ethos of moving fast, there was not sufficient time to understand the problem and mock up a thoughtful solution, and there was certainly no time to prepare for what we were about to see and hear. As we showed our mock-ups to a number of different people, there was similarly no acknowledgment or moment to share that we might have found this challenging, if not outright harrowing. I'm not suggesting that "it's all about me," but when the goal we are reaching for depends on empathy, we have to make space for it. We have to take care of ourselves first so that we can take care of others.

This is a troubling example for some researchers, who feel that it's their job to be sympathetic and to fail to do so is cold. I disagree strongly and would make the same choice again. More recently, a woman I was meeting with, after an intense two hours of discussing her paths and her goals, began to reflect on what she was grateful for. She articulated, perhaps for the first time, something deeply profound and personal. It was the highest truth about her beliefs and values, and it made me reflect on my own life and what I'm grateful for. Her honesty induced a reaction in me that I was utterly unprepared for. I thought for a moment that I might cry, and I had to work hard to keep my face straight and my voice even; to reveal my emotions would have made the dynamic about me more than her.

There's often a sense in user research that the emotional stuff is outside our scope (after all, we're here to learn about how you use our product!), and that the interview topic shouldn't drift outside those lines. Susan Simon Daniels, Kavita Appachu, and Jen Ignacz in their stories each have to deal with inadvertently treading upon emotional sore spots and their own uncertainty in how to proceed respectfully and compassionately. Whitney Hess undertakes her own journey when a highly emotional research experience shakes her deeply. Each of these researchers is guided by the strength and quality of their characters, but they reflect here on the uncertainty they face in doing so.

There are the emotions our participants express and what we do with that. And there are the emotions we experience and what we do with that. Of course, they are deeply related to each other. We have a great deal of choice around our reactions and actions and these are worth examining and learning from.

Emotions at Work: What We Can Learn from a Psychiatric Case Manager

Anne Williams

Case Manager, Inpatient Psychiatry at Kaiser Permanente

As someone who works with people who are in the hospital because of mental health or addiction issues, there can be a lot of emotion in my work. The patients I work with probably didn't choose to be in the hospital. Maybe the police were called to their house after a 911 call because they tried to hurt themselves. Or they might have been driven to the emergency room by their family because they'd been awake for days and now they were seeing and hearing things that weren't really there. Maybe they used drugs or alcohol and tried to harm someone. In situations like this, the person is likely to be admitted to a psychiatric unit of a hospital.

This can be a challenging and stressful time for the patient and the family. Sometimes the patients are upset or angry that they are in the hospital. Family members can be frustrated with their loved ones and not sure how best to help them. Both patients and families have stories they want to tell that can be very emotional. Listening to their stories brings up different emotions for me, as well.

I have to find a way to deal with these emotions. If I get a call from a family member, telling me that their loved one is doing worse and headed for the hospital, I feel my heart sink, especially if this has happened before. I can acknowledge to myself that I feel sad or disappointed or frustrated, but I don't want to express those feelings aloud to the patient or the family. That wouldn't be helpful to them. I need to listen and acknowledge *their* feelings, saying things like "Yes that must be very frustrating" or "I hear that you're feeling helpless right now." This technique of "active listening" is helpful—paraphrasing and restating both the feelings and words that I hear them saying. This helps them feel heard and understood. It also helps me to remain really present and focused on what the person is saying and the emotions behind what they are saying. I try to see things from their frame of reference and not mine. In this way, I feel more helpful and effective, and I'm not just thinking of a quick solution or an answer.

continues on next page

It helps me to quietly acknowledge my own feelings (to myself) so that I can recognize them in others. If I feel sad, I imagine how sad the patient and family must feel. If I feel frustrated during a phone conversation, I can guess that the other person must be frustrated, too.

There are formal and informal systems in place that help my co-workers and me do well in this highly emotional work context. We have regular meetings where we commonly share not only the details of a case but also our feelings about it. It's helpful to be able to talk about feelings we have about our patients—sometimes, we can be frustrated or feel inadequate about the work we're doing with them. Other times, we feel (good) sharing happy feelings about a particular patient who is doing well.

Informally, I talk with colleagues—sometimes a funny email from a co-worker can help pull me out of a sad moment. Sometimes hearing from a colleague about something similar that they went through can be especially heartening.

In addition, we're encouraged to have a balanced life—our manager wants us to use our vacation time and to work reasonable hours in order to avoid burnout. I feel supported in making sure that I take care of myself so that I can work effectively with our clients. If I'm feeling tired, stressed, or distracted, I find that I'm not as good at listening empathically or being patient with our clients. And that makes a big difference.

When I was studying social work and just beginning to work with "real" clients, I remember feeling overwhelmed by listening to stories that were sad or painful. I had the idea that if I could teach myself not to "feel" so much or to somehow shut off my emotions that I would be a more effective social worker. I remember running this idea by my father who is a psychologist. He told me just the opposite, in fact—that if you aren't feeling anything, you aren't being effective or helping at all. He said that it's recognizing and acknowledging our own feelings that makes us work more effectively with the emotions of our clients.

After working in this field for many years now, I find that this advice still holds true.

Susan Simon Daniels: A Sigh Is Just a Sigh

In September 2012, I was interviewing people who had recently purchased and set up a smartphone. During the interview, I asked the participants to unbox and set up another, new smartphone to see if any usability problems emerged.

One of the interviews was with a male in his late 40s who worked as a translator for people whose first language was not English. (I'll call him "Rick.") As he unpacked the box that contained the new smartphone, Rick frowned and sighed. I watched silently and noted that a few moments later Rick sighed again.

At this point, the researcher inside my brain was shouting, "Red alert! There's a problem! There's a problem!" After a few more moments, I turned to him and said, "Rick, I noticed you're frowning a bit, and you've sighed a couple of times. Can you tell me why?"

I waited, fingers poised to capture the fatal flaw that the participant had discovered in the product setup—something so egregious that it evoked a heavy sigh!

Rick turned to me and instead shared a personal story. Both he and his spouse had recently lost their parents. These major life events, complicated by delays in traveling to another continent for funerals and family arrangements, left a lingering sadness that crept up on Rick during quiet moments.

His sigh was just a sigh—not a signal of a defect or usability issue to solve, but a personal moment I happened to witness. We talked for a few minutes about his loss and how he was feeling, and then Rick returned to the task at hand and continued to unbox and set up the phone.

We had passed through an awkward moment. I felt I had rudely probed into an open wound. But I had to ask the question. I couldn't assume the frown and sighs were caused by the product or process. My job was to get to the *why*. At the same time, by taking a few minutes to let the person share how he was feeling, I was able to give Rick the time he needed to gather himself together and continue with the task at hand.

In the end, Rick contributed by uncovering a couple of areas of improvement for the product. And I found that taking a moment to pause, to just be human beings who shared a bit of sympathy, allowed us to resume the interview with dignity and purpose.

I'm reminded of a verse from the song "As Time Goes By" (music and lyrics by Herman Hupfeld) from the classic war-romance movie *Casablanca*.

You must remember this
A kiss is just a kiss, a sigh is just a sigh.
The fundamental things apply
As time goes by.

And the fundamental things do apply: never assume and always ask "why?"

Whitney Hess: Stories of War

I interviewed Holocaust survivors. Four words that still send shivers down my spine. Their stories were meant to shape my research; they ended up shaping me.

It was the project of a lifetime. I was asked to conduct user research for the United States Holocaust Memorial Museum with the web design agency Happy Cog. Together, we identified several constituents of the Museum to explore: visitors, students, teachers, scholars, activists, volunteers, donors ... and survivors. Survivors of the Holocaust. I would be performing the interviews, crafting personas, and reporting on findings to the Museum's executive board.

As a rule, when I engage with a research participant, I, Whitney Hess, cease to exist. It is a skill I have honed over many years of conducting research. I don't get hungry; I don't get tired; I don't have to pee. I shed my beliefs and my assumptions and my identity. My only need is to listen. My only purpose is to absorb—with total objectivity.

Would it be possible then for me to objectively study Holocaust survivors? I am a Jew.

At first I told myself that being Jewish somehow qualified me to understand their stories and empathize with their pain. Then I feared that I would get so emotional that I wouldn't be able to make it through an interview.

I was wrong on both counts.

I had the honor and the privilege of interviewing seven survivors—from Germany, Lithuania, Czechoslovakia, Austria, Poland, Slovakia, and Great Britain—all volunteers at the Holocaust Museum in varying capacities. Some interviews were in person at the Museum; others were over the phone. They shared their stories of survival, and they shared their feedback on the website. Both extremes were just as relevant. I listened with reverence, and I asked probing questions. I was so busy taking it all in, I didn't have time to feel anything about it. I was working.

When it came to crafting personas, I started with the teachers and students, moved on to activists and scholars, and eventually I could postpone it no longer—it was time to review my findings from the survivors.

Reading back through my notes and the interview transcripts, I maintained my composure. I kept reminding myself, *You have work to do.* But in a moment of weakness, I allowed myself to listen to a recording. And then another. Day became night, and I was still listening. They recounted the abuse they'd endured, the brutality they'd witnessed, the family they'd lost … it was so raw, so real. I let myself go. I cried, bawled. For what they had overcome, for themselves, for their families, and for me.

In the end, I decided not to create a persona of a survivor, and my teammates and clients understood my reasoning. Their stories were unique; they could not be merged.

Instead, I gleaned a few key quotes, to convey the essence of the individuals. What they had to say changed my whole perspective on what we were doing and why we were doing it. Their message had to be heard. I had to share it. I *got* to share it.

And it changed everything.

Kavita Appachu: Managing Money, Oh Joy!

Finance has never been my thing, and where possible I leave the chore of managing my finances to others. That changed somewhat a few years back when I started working for a company that makes financial software, specifically tax software. This threw me right in the middle of people's financial lives.

What I had not realized was that while the task of managing finances may be very functional, everything else related to money and taxes is at its core very emotional. I have lost track of the innumerable times participants have poured their hearts out as they describe how they manage their finances, from the twenty-something who referred to her mom as *ghetto*, or the hulk of a guy who rattled off the choicest of expletives for his ex-wife. The one story that has stood out in all this is about a mom, wife, and editor in Seattle.

On a rare sunny day, we pulled up to a community of condos with well-manicured yards. We rang the doorbell, and my fellow researcher and I were greeted by our participant, who welcomed us into her very tastefully done home. There were pictures of the kids, family vacations, sporting events. It seemed like a happy home. The kids were at school and our participant had the morning off so she had decided to catch up on her finances, specifically her investments. We talked about the members of her household, her husband's job, her job, and their approach to financial planning. She was concerned their savings were not going to be enough for retirement and the kids' education.

She had all her papers spread out on the dining table beside her laptop. We observed her going through the process of logging into both her and her husband's 401(k) accounts, monitoring her mutual funds and stocks and even placing a sell order. Nothing out of the ordinary . . . and then she broke down in tears.

We were a little taken aback. She had a helpless look on her face and kept sobbing and muttering *that woman, that woman*. We calmed her down and then asked her if she wanted to share what was bothering her. She told us that as part of her husband's divorce settlement from his earlier marriage, he was required to pay for her stepchildren's college. That was making a deep hole in their pockets, and she was unable to save for her own children's college education, take vacations, or save for retirement. She hated the ex-wife and held her husband somewhat responsible for giving in to the ex-wife's demands. She avoided tracking finances if she could because it was a painful reminder of her dire situation.

That was my *aha* moment. I had known all along that personal finances are very closely entwined to one's life, but this experience really brought it home: personal finances are a mirror of your inner joys, sorrows, and insecurities.

Jen Ignacz: Bad News Turns to Couples Therapy

I was conducting in-home contextual interviews about home safety and security behaviors. In the recruitment screener, I had discovered that a particular participant had experienced a break-in to her home about a year earlier.

When I arrived at her home for the interview, her fiancé was also there and ended up participating extensively in the conversation.

My research partner and I had been with the couple for about 90 minutes, and they were obviously feeling quite comfortable; they offered lots of intimate details about their routines and behaviors and were willing to show us everything and anything. I was pleased that they felt so comfortable with sharing (the woman more than the man).

Part of my protocol was to understand what happened when people found out about bad news about their home, like a fire alarm going off, a break-in, a water leak, etc. So, after 90 minutes of talking about home safety and security routines, I posed the question: "Now I want to talk about what you do when you get bad news. You mentioned that you had a break-in last year. Can you tell me about what happened?"

As I was asking, the couple looked at each other and an awkward silence fell over the room as I finished the question. They held each other's gaze for longer than was comfortable (for us). Their sudden change in behavior told me I had hit a sore spot.

The woman broke the silence, still holding her partner's gaze, saying, "That's not what I consider bad news. Your child dying is bad news." Then a whispered "Do you not want to talk about this?" to her fiancé.

My research partner and I froze, as if hoping that by not moving, time could stand still for us while they dealt with this incredibly intense personal moment.

The couple started to talk about the experience of losing a pregnancy in the second trimester about a year earlier. (I made the discovery when reviewing the recordings that the break-in had happened around the same time as the miscarriage, so asking the question the way I did allowed for a connection between events I could not have anticipated.) They spoke quietly and mostly to each other, but engaged me more and more in their conversation as they went along.

As a researcher, this felt *way* off-topic, and I was trying to think of ways to get the interview back on track. But as a human being, I felt the need to let them deal with this issue that seemed difficult for them to talk about. From their conversation, it was quite clear they each were still working through their emotions and likely didn't speak about it to each other often enough. I wasn't going to shut down an opportunity for them to make emotional progress just because it didn't fit anywhere close to my research goals.

So I let them talk. And I even guided them to share some feelings with each other. I took on a counseling role—a total deviation from the research plan.

After about ten minutes, they turned to me and said, "That's probably not what you meant."

I was honest with them. I told them it wasn't the type of bad news event I was thinking about, but the conversation helped me learn more about who they were: their values, morals, and perspectives on life. Getting a better sense of who they were ultimately helped me understand their motives for their behaviors better.

My response allowed us to carefully ramp back up to the interview protocol. I was very cautious with that transition. I had to ensure that the trust and openness we had established in the first 90 minutes wasn't harmed by the unexpectedly exposed vulnerability. It didn't seem to be. I was able to complete the remaining hour of the visit with just as much openness (and gaining just as much insight) as we had before.

Takeaways

- **You can't choose how you feel, but you do choose how to act and how not to act.** You shouldn't default to the same choices in an interview setting that you would in a social setting.

- **Listening is supporting.** You can support your participants by listening to them deeply. It's possible that no one else in their life is doing that for them. This can be more powerful—and more appropriate for your research—than expressions of concern.

- **Emotion isn't a bad thing.** Allow for the possibility of tears, even tears of sadness. You needn't aim for tears, but you should be okay if it happens. Whether you steer into or away from the area of sadness depends on the specifics.

- **Prepare to be triggered.** You may keenly feel your own joy, grief, anxiety, gratitude, etc. when a participant talks about theirs. Keeping in touch with your own emotions, especially when you are in the field, can help you compartmentalize during the interview. Acknowledge your own feelings and set them aside for the time being.

- **Give your emotions an opportunity to surface.** If you feel like crying during an interview, that doesn't mean that you need to burst into tears in front of colleagues the moment you step outside the interview. It may be safer to simply acknowledge your feelings, saying, "I felt like crying when he told us about ..." Acknowledging the emotion, aloud, to another person, especially someone who shared the experience, is good for you, and will make it easier to go into the next interview. Look for a more private time later where you can sigh deeply, and if you still feel the need, cry.

- **We meet people wherever they are at in life**. Don't assume the emotion you observe is about you or your product.

- **While you have research objectives as the presumptive topics for the interview, that is not how your participant thinks about the interview.** Give yourself permission to veer from your set of questions and even your underlying assumptions as to what you "should" be talking about. This can provide a richer understanding of your participant and shed light on the deeper issues that inform your objectives.

The Myth of Objectivity

Photo by Steve Portigal

In our culture in general, we place a high premium on the notion of objectivity. We hold high the values of fairness and neutrality. Journalists frequently face the criticism of bias. But the endeavors of law, news, science, and user research are led by humans. Unlike Vulcans, humans are not wholly led by logic. The field of behavioral economics, increasingly totemic for business people of all stripes, seeks to understand the ways in which people's behaviors and decisions are influenced by irrational factors.

The field of science has long understood this about people, establishing the practice of blind experiments in the 1700s. In blind experiments, the subjects who received different conditions didn't know what those conditions were. Starting in 1907 and fully established by the 1950s, the double-blind experiment goes even further. In a double-blind experiment, neither the subjects nor the experimenters know what the conditions are.

Consider the scientist who is trying to determine the efficacy of a new drug: some subjects receive the new drug; others receive a placebo. In a blind experiment, the subjects don't know what they've received. In a double-blind experiment, the subjects don't know, but neither does the scientist. It makes intuitive sense that the subject would report different effects based on their assumptions about what they were given, but it goes farther—knowledge of the drug they received (or did not receive) could also manifest in physical signs, such as pulse, blood pressure, or reaction times. But the double-blind goes farther still—to ensure that the subject doesn't have this knowledge, the scientist herself doesn't even know. This protocol doesn't presume that the scientist would ever reveal details to the subject, rather it eliminates the possibility of the scientist unknowingly and unconsciously signaling crucial information through body language, tone of voice, or choice of words. It also ensures that the scientist won't be influenced to ignore symptoms or patient complaints or emphasize one type of reading over another.

That's how powerful bias is and how extensively the practice of science is structured to minimize it. In user research, we bring in our own subjectivity toward the outcomes, such as the expectations and aspirations of our clients and stakeholders, our emerging hypotheses, etc. And that's just only one flavor of bias, experimental and otherwise, that we must be cautious of in user research.

In this chapter, we're going to look more deeply at a specific challenge to our objectivity—that as humans we are not only flawed, irrational, emotional, and judging beings, but we are also individuals who are the result of our accumulated life experiences. As Trekkers will know, it's not that the Vulcans didn't have emotions, it was that as a society they chose to actively control them in favor of logic. Like the Vulcans, there is no denying who each of us is and the paths we've gone down. And like the Vulcans, there is no easy path to work through the challenges to our own values and beliefs.

You'll read how researchers grappled with challenges to their own values, experiences, and circumstances. Gregory Cabrera spent time in an Afghan village, Raffaella Roviglioni met a farmer who had his own ideas about who she was, Marta Guy went into a chaotic household and reacted differently than her colleagues, and Priya Sohoni visited a maternity ward while pregnant.

While these researchers did not achieve an unrealistic level of objectivity, we don't fault them. They relate here how they each encountered, acknowledged, and addressed the ways that the world outside differed from the way they might have imagined it would be. Of course, this is the inevitable consequence of stepping outside, and indeed it's why we do this work, to find out the ways the world differs from our own assumptions. The musician Neil Young talked about how he experienced this in his own career: "'Heart of Gold' put me in the middle of the road. Traveling there soon became a bore, so I headed for the ditch. A rougher ride but I saw more interesting people there."[1]

These stories surface a crucial question for user researchers: When you stride forward past the borderlands of your own worldview, what will you do with what you find? What will you do when you see or hear or experience something that challenges your own personal values? This is well beyond hearing that someone doesn't believe your product's new feature is compelling. These challenges to your personal values are, well, very personal. A great researcher doesn't let them bounce off, they process them and if they are very lucky and very good, they can also put that back into the work itself.

---

1 Liner notes to Neil Young's *Decade*

Dak Kopec, Ph.D.

Research is about the process of discovery and gaining further insights about a given situation or phenomenon. To gain the most from research findings, you must first understand some of the fundamental concepts that underpin all research. One important concept is that all research can be invalidated by biases. Biases in research can occur during the formation of research goals, development of tools used to gather responses, during the gathering of information, and when communicating the results.

All research begins with an idea that a researcher would like to explore. This should come from an inquisitive desire to learn more, but sometimes your personal passions or beliefs overshadow the research. This commonly happens in one of two ways.

- Confirmation bias occurs when a researcher promotes their beliefs in the research. This occurs when the researcher is too close to the subject matter or has an invested interest in the outcome.

- Culture bias occurs when the researcher's cultural lens is projected onto the research. This happens when the researcher stereotypes a group, or imposes their own beliefs and values onto another group.

Once a researcher has been able to set aside their own beliefs and values, and can fully understand and empathize with the subject population, the researcher can take the next step. The development of a tool to gather information may introduce biases. Some of the biases related to the research tool include:

- Question-order bias, which is when the ordering of questions in the tool predetermines or influences the responses in subsequent questions. The idea behind this bias is that the researcher can set a tone with their questions, and can thus influence the subjects' responses.

- Leading questions and wording bias is exactly what it states. It occurs when a researcher uses vocal tone, helps respondents finish their sentences, or uses leading questions to promote a desired outcome.

Once a research tool has been developed, it needs to be administered to a sample pool of subjects. Just as the researcher can bias the results, so can the subjects. These biases can be minimized if you know what to look for and how to manage them. Subject-driven biases can come from:

- Acquiescence bias occurs when the subject says what they think the researcher wants to hear to "get it over."

- Social desirability bias happens when the subject answers the way they think will bring about greater acceptance from the researcher.

- Habituation happens when subjects provide the same answers to questions that are worded in similar ways. This happens because respondents are unaware of subtle differences.

- Sponsor bias happens when the subjects have an idea of the purpose, or the sponsor, of the research and wish to promote a particular agenda.

- The halo effect happens when the researcher or respondent reacts to a physical trait or aspect that influences the responses or interpretation of the responses. The halo effect usually happens when the subject wants to please the researcher, but can also result from a fear evoked by a physical trait (i.e., a man wearing a tie).

The final stage of research involves the interpretation of data and characterization of that data. There are two ways in which research findings can be biased:

- Overgeneralization is the application of research findings beyond the actual research. An example of overgeneralization occurs when the research findings apply to Granny Smith apples, but the researcher speaks of the findings in relation to golden delicious apples. Just because they are both apples doesn't mean the research is applicable.

- Misrepresentation pertains to the depiction of data, or failing to disclose limitations. Misrepresentation of data can occur when the researchers choose to use percentiles without the use of whole numbers. Seventy percent of 10 is only seven. However, seventy percent is more compelling than seven. Misrepresentation can also come from not identifying limitations, which might include the tool only being offered to select subjects, only during select times, or only using non-probability sampling techniques (cherry-picking the subjects).

The majority of biases in research are unintentional and come from a lack of experience. Biases can present with quantitative and qualitative approaches and can affect the internal and external validity of the research data. When biases occur, the reliability comes into question. However, biases can be avoided.

One way to avoid bias is to ask a third party to review the research goals and tools. If the researcher informs the third-party reviewer of their personal beliefs and values, the reviewer will be better equipped to know what to look for. After careful construction of the research tool, the researcher will need to pay careful attention to the subjects and their responses. The researcher must be prepared to eliminate data that they suspect was biased by the subject. To avoid biases in the presentation of results, the key is to disclose. If it seems like additional information should be disclosed, then it should. Good research is hard to accomplish, but careful consideration and attention can make the research solid and provide good information.

Gregory Cabrera: Culture Shock

One of the first places I visited in Afghanistan was a security checkpoint along a major route in northern Kandahar. The security was contracted to a private group of Afghans, mainly from the south and east, to provide route security and protect military and civilian supply routes. Their job was to protect the route against insurgents who wanted to disrupt the convoy and see oil tankers burn.

A few days before insurgents did exactly this. They stopped a convoy carrying military supplies by using an improvised explosive device (IED), hitting the first truck and killing the driver. Then they attacked the last truck and shot a rocket-propelled grenade, which effectively exploded and hit the side of a fuel truck. Civilians fled, the insurgents attacked the checkpoint, and it was utter chaos. These security guards returned fire and called the local police for reinforcements. All that was left at the end were a few burned trucks, dead bodies, and some burned firearms.

Upon arrival, I could see where these men were being shot at, how they fought back, and where they stored their weapons. They worked on this mountain and lived here, too. There were approximately 15 to 20 men living in this bunker. All they carried were machine guns, assault rifles, ammunition, and blankets. Of course, they also had food, chai, cooking supplies, and utensils. As I inspected their site and positions, they told me about the event and shared their war trophies, burned AK-47s captured from insurgents. It was unusual to observe so many men living in such a tight area together, away from their villages and homes. This was security, Afghan style, and it felt like a group of armed nomads living under the radar. They were living and working together in a confined space in the middle of what felt like nowhere in particular. I would later find out that these men often worked for two to three months at a time before going home for a short period.

When we all sat down for chai, I noticed some of the people who were working at this checkpoint did not look old enough to be here. I thought to myself "Shouldn't these kids be riding their bikes or playing in the village?" The individual who was serving chai and placing candies out for our consumption did not have facial hair and had henna-painted fingers and toenails. I looked over at my interpreter and asked him on the side what these kids were doing here hanging out with security guards. My interpreter, looking down, smiled, and turned to me saying, "They have fun with them at night."

PHOTOS BY GREGORY CABRERA

The sergeant whom I worked with was sitting across from me. When he heard this, his face turned blank. I could tell this made him uneasy. I always wondered what the expression on my face looked like. As the young boy finished serving everyone chai, he moved near an older male who was resting comfortably on a pillow on his side. That's weird, I thought to myself. I had just arrived in-country, at this field site, surrounded by strange men who did strange things. I grabbed my cup of chai and drank it down.

Despite the weirdness of the situation, I carried on. I asked lots of questions, took lots of notes, and attempted to be as respectful of their culture as possible, even though it bothered me and made me uncomfortable. Who was I to judge? I wondered to myself, what business did we as a nation have in this country? How can its people allow human exploitation to exist like this? I learned later on that Kandahar was a different place than most of Afghanistan. It retained practices unlike the rest of the country. Although this specific instance of culture shock made me uneasy to say the least, I learned to see past it. This was an unconventional war in a strange, neglected land, and I was not there to change their culture, only study it.

Raffaella Roviglioni: Learning to Deal with Expectations

I'm currently a freelance UX designer based in Rome, Italy, but I used to be an agronomist. I like to see my professional shift not as a mutation but rather as an evolution. I understood that my passion was working with people, and now user research and UX work is fulfilling that need. Despite the different context and purpose that drove me as an agronomist, I had to interview people quite often, and I didn't have any formal training in it. I guess I was attracted to this kind of activity because I'm an outgoing person and consider myself to be a good listener.

Back in the days when I was a research fellow at the University of Viterbo, I was involved in a pretty interesting project: investigating the old fruit tree varieties in my region. Part of the job (for me the most exciting part!) was interviewing old farmers who were between 80 and 90 years old; they were both the guardians of those old plants and the living repository of the related knowledge.

The job required me to travel to their houses and farms to perform the interviews. Given the distance and the remote location of the rural areas, the best way of getting there was by car. As a research fellow, though, I wasn't allowed to drive the department car, since I wasn't considered to be an actual employee, according to Italian law.

PHOTO BY RAFFAELLA ROVIGLIONI

A lab assistant (also a good friend of mine) agreed to come with me on the field trips. He was basically acting as my driver, but helped out with taking pictures and collecting plant samples in the field.

It was during a first visit to one farmer's house that the unexpected happened.

We arrived, got out of the car, and went over to the farmer who was waiting for us at the front door. He greeted my assistant first, and then looked at me and said to him, "So this must be your wife!" Even after an embarrassed explanation from our side, he clearly could not believe I was the one in charge of the research (with a college degree!) whereas my friend was "only" my assistant.

I have to confess that at first I had to rationalize a bit not to feel offended by his reaction. But after all, I told myself, he was over 80 years old, and even my grandfather would have had the same reaction in a similar situation. But the awkwardness continued because, given the context, this farmer wouldn't expect me to conduct the interview either!

So what I did instead was direct us all (the farmer, his wife, my assistant, and me) to have coffee together, inside the house. We started chatting while drinking our coffee, as any pair of couples would do. Slowly I moved the conversation to the questions on the plants we were interested in. This allowed us to establish a more acceptable situation where the farmer felt comfortable enough to start sharing that information.

What I learned from this experience was that in order to ensure my interview was successful I needed to be able to deal with the expectations of others, embracing them and trying to let go of my emotions (as in this instance, avoiding feeling offended). I also realized that as an interviewer I needed to adapt to the interviewee's setup (in this case, transforming what I view as *an interview* to *a visit to the house*) and act accordingly.

It wasn't my first interview, nor the last, but it taught me a lot!

Marta Guy: On Confronting Judgment

I was fresh out of the Peace Corps. With an educational background in photography and videography and a unique set of personal contacts, somehow I landed a contracting gig at a design strategy firm. It turned out this was the perfect place for me. It made sense that all roads led here, although I wasn't able to articulate why at that time. My experiences on that first project would solidify both my approach to ethnographic-style research and my interest in innovation in the business sector. The techniques and tasks associated with international development shared some remarkable similarities with those we utilize in business innovation and design strategy today.

In our Peace Corps training, we were encouraged to "do nothing" for the first six months of our service—to just sit with the host-country nationals in their day-to-day activities, and observe and ask questions. Indeed, most of my Peace Corps experience was composed of these moments of quiet observation, learning about a culture so foreign to me as to deeply challenge my own beliefs. In both international development and strategic design, this anthropological approach to learning about the people we're designing for is the foundation of an often ambiguous process to create new concepts that will be adopted by people like those whom we've studied and ideally help improve their lives.

Although I had mostly casual experience doing this as a Peace Corps volunteer, an incident occurred when I was on my first professional foray into ethnographic-style user research. Our team was learning about people's experiences using medical devices in the home. At this point, we had spoken with a couple of dozen people, including medical practitioners in their professional settings and patients in their homes. We were on our final interview of the study. My role had been to photograph and video the interviews, take notes, and generally follow the lead of my teammates who were directing the sessions. But for this final interview, my colleagues asked if I'd like to conduct the conversation, and I took them up on the opportunity to lead my first formal in-context interview.

We drove to a relatively remote location in Connecticut to see a middle-class family of two parents and three boys. Two of the boys had an immune condition that required them to pump medication for one to two hours every two weeks. The parents had decided that rather than stigmatize or devitalize the process of the boys' drug infusion, they would celebrate it by joining together as a family for a pizza party and movies on Friday night. This celebration was in full swing when we entered their home.

It was a lively atmosphere. It turned out this wasn't just a family of five; they lived with a menagerie of animals in their small home: cats, dogs, birds, rabbits, reptiles, and guinea pigs, all in all between 20 and 30 inhabitants. We were introduced to the guinea pigs and shown the rabbits. Everyone was supremely generous and inviting. They gave us a little tour and encouraged us to get comfortable, offering us food and drink several times. Cats snuggled up beside us, intermittently disrupting our video equipment or the conversation, while birds squawked in the background. Comfortable and confident among one another, this family moved freely and raucously around me and my two colleagues, all squished onto too few pieces of furniture for eight humans.

The parents graciously answered our questions about their children's health and medical needs. Meanwhile, the boys played video games and watched cartoons energetically, occasionally peppering the conversation with commentary or boisterous requests for attention—"Watch this! Watch!" The parents showed us how they hooked up the medication pumps, from prepping their sons' skin to inserting the needles. The father proudly brought out two large toolboxes full of medical supplies that they took along whenever they got in the car.

He had come up with the idea of creating toolkits for the supplies they needed to be mobile. The interview continued successfully, if a bit disordered, given all the different activities happening. Not at any moment were they embarrassed or ashamed of the boys' condition or the things they had to do to treat it. To them, this was just their life.

When we finally said good-bye, and the door shut behind us, I think all three of us researchers breathed a sigh of relief. Truthfully, it had all been quite chaotic, though we had done our best to take it in stride. But our last interview was complete, and we got into the car, heading toward New York to fly home the next day.

Driving along, one of my teammates offhandedly said, "Well, I don't think we learned anything useful from that. That scene was a complete mess! What a waste of time." This thoughtless comment infuriated me. Sure, the situation was intense, chaotic, and a less tidy environment than we might have desired. They had more animal friends than a small farmer might, and the lifestyle this family lived was obviously busy and disorganized. Certainly, they had some health problems, probably some difficulty making ends meet, and a shortage of square footage for all of the living things in their home. But they also clearly loved one another and were just doing the best they could to live full, healthy, and enjoyable lives. I might have been totally green and unfamiliar with conducting research for new business innovation, but I knew it wasn't our place to judge, whether we approved of their lifestyle or not.

I was so angry. Never one to hold back, I told this teammate exactly what I thought—that these people had generously invited us into their home so that we might learn about how they lived, how they experienced their medical conditions, and how they interacted with these essential medical devices. Whether we found their lifestyle appealing or disgusting, it was valid. Their experiences were real, and we were there to learn about them. It was unfair and totally inappropriate to judge them, and it missed the entire point of what we were there to do. I said all this, I'm sure, not nearly as eloquently as I say it now, and likely with less respect than my colleague deserved, as he had more experience and knowledge on the subject than I did. He actually took it relatively well, all things considered, and we remain friends today despite the words exchanged on that trip.

I've found this to be one of the formative moments of my career, a moment when I expressed with passion and understanding just exactly what our purpose was there. And I've found similar sentiments coming to my lips again and again (with increasing grace and respect, of course), as I've had to remind most often clients but sometimes colleagues why we do this work. For an hour or two, we go into the home of a stranger, with a respect and appreciation for the validity of each individual's experience. We must practice empathy, reserving judgment, allowing ourselves to stand in the other's shoes, understand how he lives, why she does what she does, what they want to achieve and what makes that hard for them. So that in the end we might create better solutions that help them do it and make theirs and other people's lives better and healthier. Sometimes, we just have to remind ourselves.

Priya Sohoni: Taking Empathy to a Whole New Level

I've never been too comfortable with hospital environments—the smells, sounds, sense of urgency—it makes me nervous. Yet, as an ethnographer should, I've attempted to conquer my queasiness and conduct research in medical facilities several times.

In October 2010, I was conducting research in a hospital in the San Francisco Bay area. I was almost eight months pregnant with my first child. I was given a choice between spending a day in the ICU, emergency, or the maternity department. I picked maternity—I was excited to be among so many about-to-pop mothers and so many who had just delivered. I thought to myself that for the first time I wasn't feeling so queasy. I could hear babies in nurseries, and we shadowed some nurses as they took the babies for their first immunizations, observed visitors greeting happy families with flowers, balloons, gifts ... it seemed so odd that this was a part of a "hospital" environment.

On one of the shadowing sessions, I sat in on a nurse shift change. The nurses went around the table sharing information about the newborns and their mothers and taking careful notes of the patients' needs and requests. On one of the nurse's share-outs, she turned to the nursing manager and said, "Baby girl in room 203, born vaginally at 8:02 a.m., had trouble breathing, survived for 53 seconds, and then died. Should I register her as a live birth or a still birth?" I felt as if someone had stabbed me in my stomach. So much pain that I clenched my tummy, sat down on the floor, and burst into tears. I was expecting a baby girl, too, in just over a month. Why was the nurse so unemotional about a baby's death? The nursing manager noticed me sitting in the corner, brought me a glass of water, and apologized that I had to sit through that. She suggested I take some rest in the nurses' break room. But I wiped my tears away and stuck around.

PHOTO BY PRIYA SOHONI

In a few more minutes, the shift change was over, and the nurses dispersed. The nurse from 203 then walked over to another room to check in on another mother and her baby. I continued shadowing her. She entered the room with a big smile on her face, congratulated the parents, and commented on what a beautiful baby they had. She changed the baby, swaddled her, gave the mother her meds, and assured her that she could call for help whenever she felt like it. It then struck me that the nurse was concerned about her patients. Deeply concerned. She, too, had felt the pain that the family in room 203 had gone through. But she had made a commitment to hundreds of other patients, a commitment to take care of them and make them feel better. She could not have done that if she had carried the sorrow with her, out of room 203.

As ethnographers, we are trained to empathize with our respondents. To speak their language, to make them comfortable, to be one of them. I had just witnessed a remarkable new level of empathy that the nurse had. Where I had failed, she carried out each one of her roles with respect and propriety.

I went home that day with a new appreciation for the nursing profession.

Takeaways

- **Know yourself.** Awareness of who you are and what you believe in can make these encounters less precarious. You can simply note that this person or situation is different from you. Indeed, that can be valuable data!

- **Feeling judgment isn't the same as acting on it.** Fieldwork is a series of choices. You may feel disturbed, surprised, offended (or thrilled, overjoyed, delighted), but you don't have to expressly state your feelings nor (to the extent possible) default to having them guide your actions. Learn to identify that feeling when it starts creeping up on you.

- **Work in teams.** Interviews work best with a team of two. Those two may react similarly or differently to any particular situation; in either case, it's valuable to have each other to debrief with. By the same token, having different teams conducting interviews also means you have access to different perspectives among the different sessions.

- **When debriefing, talk about what you feel, not just what you see or infer.** Of course, it's good for us as people to process our feelings as a way to take care of ourselves, but it's also good for the research. What you feel influences what you see and hear, so talk about it to unpack your insights as part of your own unique perspective.

Conclusion

—Ira Glass[1]

Going out into the world to learn from people is risky. No matter how curious we are, we don't know what we don't know. And no matter how prepared we are, we don't know what will happen. These challenging experiences change us and serve as a source for greater learning about our users and ourselves. While not every venture out into the field results in a war story (thankfully), anyone doing research will begin to accumulate stories. These stories provide an opportunity for discussion and debate. We bring our own perspective as readers, and we may not agree with the choices the author made in the field, or how they feel about what happened. Some of the most valuable learning from these stories can come from considering them from different perspectives. Reflect on these stories yourself or get together with others and talk about the stories. See the Discussion Guide[2] on page 211 for suggested questions and topics to help you reflect and grow.

These war stories reaffirm the humanity at the very root of user research. The people doing research are human, and the people we want to learn from are human. I use the word "human" as a proxy for the many qualities that lead to these stories: emotional, vulnerable, unpredictable, flawed, ambitious, error-prone, insecure, curious, patient, judgmental, messy, anxious, persistent, reflective, thoughtful, and kind. These stories teach us that researchers are always learning to do research and that learning goes beyond a set of methods—we must grapple with ourselves as humans in a world of humans.

You probably have stories. Your colleagues have stories. Tell these stories! Whether it's over drinks (the delightful war story cliché), or in a workshop-style setting, just tell them. Write them up! Publish them yourself or submit them to the archive. The more we share stories of failure, the more we normalize thoughtful and transparent consideration of our work. The storytellers here have bravely and honestly shared their own experiences. You needn't feel alone with your mistakes; instead, you can join their illustrious ranks. All it takes is a story.

---

1 Although this quote is generally attributed to Ira Glass, I couldn't find a source. Glass refutes credit for the phrase, referring to it in one interview as "the old adage."

2 http://rfld.me/DiscGuid

- Set the context right away. Describe where and when the story takes place and explain briefly what the research was about.

- Remember you are writing a story about the researcher, not the research. You aren't reporting on results; you are sharing a single thing that happened to you.

- Your story needs a beginning, a middle, and an end. While your impetus to write may start by recalling a headline (e.g., "I once met a guy who said he invented the ladder"), your story moves linearly through time and describes the entire experience.

- Stories usually have an "inciting incident"—one or several points at which the normal flow is disrupted and the story-worthy thing emerges.

- Use detail to slow down time and highlight the drama. Consider the critical moments of the story and describe those moments in great detail. Think about what it looked like, how you felt, and what you were thinking.

- You don't need a moral to your story. Resist the desire to wrap the story up in a lesson.

Let's wrap up with one more story, where a researcher felt profoundly lost out in the field, but found a way to ground himself and address the business challenge that was the reason he was out in the field to begin with.

Steve Sato: Finding Mojo in the Moment

Steve told this story live at an event in 2014.[3]

We were three days into our 18-day research trip. The clock was ticking, and our progress had been frustratingly slow. We had nary an insight to show for our time spent here so far. It was 9 o'clock in the morning, and we were already hot and sweaty after having walked a quarter of a mile on the footpath, the only way to reach a remote village in Uganda.

---

3 https://vimeo.com/141800152

Our team was doing field research on making microfinance more efficient and reliable so that banks and other financial institutions would find it profitable for them to extend their services to include microfinancing. The current system of paper and pencil, traveling back and forth to an office two hours away, and then transcribing notes onto a PC ("sneaker net") was inefficient and fraught with errors and omissions. Furthermore, what was required was not only an IT system that could span "the last mile," but we had 15 days left to prototype an interaction model that would augment the device. It needed to be a process that the field agents and their clients would trust and adopt without much help. On top of that, we had to identify what other not-for-profit and for-profit organizations (e.g., medical, agriculture, manufacturing, and so on) would find the field device useful (so we could size the potential market for the device).

I was responsible for the research and the results. I really was feeling the stress and the jet lag, and I had had heartburn nonstop from the first day there.

We arrived at the village, and our team was introduced by the microfinance agent to a group of a dozen women who were her clients. After a few minutes of conversation, the women gathered and sat down with the field agent, on the ground in a large circle. Two researchers stationed themselves behind the agent while the rest of us positioned ourselves around the perimeter of the circle. I turned on the video camera and thought "Whew! We've been prepping for this for nearly a month and now we'll finally get to make some interesting discoveries!" But then I spent the next half hour struggling to stay focused, to listen to the conversation and watch the exchange between a woman and the field agent. Then some amount of self-awareness seeped into my head: "The breeze feels so good, gosh! I'm so exhausted, I could go to sleep right now ... let me see, it's 11ish at night in Portland. ... Oh! I promised I'd call my wife today!"

Without thinking, I pulled out my cell phone and looked to see if I had a signal. To my surprise, I had one bar! By walking away from the group toward a little rise, I could get 2–3 bars, which was good enough!

It was good to hear my wife's voice. I closed my eyes while talking with her for about five minutes, like I was only a block away. I felt calm relief return.

But then my eyes popped open, because with the relief came a realization, triggered by my ability to connect to my wife halfway around the world while I'm in the African backcountry, gazing at a group of women sitting in the grass under the shade of a huge tree, with puffy white clouds against a bright blue sky. It was surreal and so powerful. I experientially understood our mission: to connect the people here to the world in a way that would make their everyday lives better, as was happening to me in the moment. Suddenly, I was re-energized and fully present. Throughout the rest of the trip, I kept going back to relive this experience. It kept me energized, engaged, and focused, no matter how exhausted I felt. I honestly believe it made a positive difference in what we discovered, what we surmised, and in our final designs.

In Memoriam
Steve Sato

PHOTO BY DIXIE MATSON

Photo by Steve Portigal

INDEX

DISCUSSION GUIDE

S tudents, book clubs, and other groups can use these questions to help facilitate discussion about a particular war story. For any particular story, some questions may be more relevant than others.

1. What were they trying to accomplish?

2. What went wrong, or what happened?

3. How did the researcher feel?

4. How would you have felt?

5. What assumptions were made about the participant?

6. What was the research participant's experience?

7. What could the researcher have done to prevent or prepare for this?

8. What could the researcher have done in the moment to address this?

9. What could the researcher have done afterward to mitigate the situation?

10. What questions do you have about the story?

11. What lessons did the researcher learn?

12. What other lessons might they have learned?

13. What experiences of your own, from research, does this bring to light?

14. What experiences of your own, from other parts of your life, does this bring to light?

Download a copy of this guide at http://rfld.me/DiscGuid

CONTRIBUTORS

Elaine Ann ("I Thought My Client Was Going to Die," Chapter 3) is the founder and CEO of Kaizor Innovation. Her consultancy helps companies strategize, research, and define innovative products and services for the China market, as well as training executives and students on new product/services innovation and user experience. Her clients range from multinationals, Asian companies, and SMEs to start-ups: Google, Airbnb, DropBox, BMW DesignworksUSA, Intel, Motorola, Siemens, Herman Miller, HP, P&G, Hyatt, Cartier, Wellington Fund, SapientNitro, iSentia, Design Continuum, and Lunar. Elaine graduated from Carnegie Mellon University with a BFA in Visual Communication Design and Master of Interaction Design. She is also an EMBA alumni of the Cheung Kong Business School (Beijing).

Kavita Appachu ("Managing Money, Oh Joy!" Chapter 10) is a seasoned user experience (UX) professional with a track record of driving UX strategy and design thinking to deliver business results for leading global brands such as TurboTax, Kelley Blue Book, AOL, and Netscape. She is passionate about collaborating cross-functionally, leveraging empathy to uncover insights to formulate innovative experiences that are unexpected and loved by customers. She currently manages UX research at Kelley Blue Book where she promotes customer immersion and the adoption of design thinking methodologies to create products that build on KBB's competitive advantage.

Lena Blackstock ("The Researcher and the Banana Thief," Chapter 7) is a senior consultant of ethnographic research and strategic design at Infosys Consulting. She is a design strategist with an ethnographic mindset and design-thinker/doer attitude. She focuses on discovering and contextualizing the mundane. Lena is fascinated by technology, nature, and humans and especially the friction points and their converging contexts. She believes in a life of experience and reflection, seeking balance of the brain, the heart, and the gut in all aspects of her life. She is a working and self-loving mom, trying to balance grace, love, energy, and time received and given in all aspects of family/work/play/self-fulfilling life. See more at www.lenacorinna.com.

David Bloxsom ("When the Work Itself Isn't Safe for Work," Chapter 6) has spent 18 years working in design, production, information architecture, user experience, and project management. Starting as a receptionist at a design firm, he went on to found their burgeoning online production department. During that time, he developed an integrated design and development process that focused on user-centered design and integrated the then-nascent field of information architecture. His most recent engagement was 11 years with an award-winning video-streaming company where he focused on content strategy and worked with specialized taxonomies and controlled vocabularies. This work would become the basis for a presentation he gave at the 2014 IA Summit entitled "Designing for Villains."

Raffaele Boiano ("The Enemy Employee," Chapter 7) finds himself juggling cultural anthropology, experience design, creative writing, and pair coding. He has 15+ years' experience shaping usable and delightful product/services experiences. His strong skill sets include user research, information architecture, user interface design, usability testing, and front-end coding. Co-founder of Fifth Beat, a design innovation boutique, he is now committed to make the world a better place. Raffaele also is an adjunct professor of UX design at Politecnico di Milano, vice president of the Italian Information Architecture Society, and co-founder of Roma's UX book club.

Carla Borsoi ("A Dirty Diaper Sitting in the Mud," Chapter 5) heads up marketing at Nima. She was formerly at AOL and Ask.com in senior roles overseeing consumer insights and marketing. She's been working in consumer-oriented technology since the late 1990s. In the course of her career, she's conducted hundreds of user interviews, formal and informal, and led large research projects focused on new product introduction, major marketing initiatives, and helping companies connect with the needs that real people have. Carla holds an ABH in Spanish and theater and an MBA, both from Rollins College. See more at www.carlaborsoi.com.

Nick Bowmast ("Diary Studies at Motorway Speed," Chapter 7) is an independent design researcher working internationally from New Zealand. He dives into the lives of consumers, to discover what matters to them, the shape of their world, and how products or services can best fit. His work helps clients discover insights for themselves, inspiring designers and business teams through visual storytelling and video. Because he's often sent by his clients to track down user needs, he became an accidental entrepreneur when he realized UX researchers needed a way to film mobile device research, which led to his product, Mr. Tappy, which does just that. Nick likes to share what he's learned from conducting thousands of hours of design research through dozens of articles at www.userexperience.co.nz. See more about his company at www.bowmast.com.

Kelly Braun ("Pictures Are Language Independent," Chapter 6) has spent her career making technology easier to use. She believes that excellence in user experience drives higher revenues and more frequent brand interactions across a wider and more diverse customer base. Her passion is identifying design solutions through user research that drives business success. Kelly is an expert at building and leading user experience research and design teams. She has built user experience teams at eBay, PayPal, and WalmartLabs. Kelly holds a BS in Computer Science from Georgia Tech and a PhD in Cognitive Psychology from Duke University. Kelly is currently on the Advisory Board for the College of Computing at Georgia Tech and is also on the Advisory Board of the Georgia Tech GVU Center.

Francoise Brun-Cottan ("Black Glances Cast Our Way," Chapter 4) was a senior research scientist who spent over a decade as a workplace ethnographer and interaction analyst with Xerox PARC (Palo Alto Research Center and Webster Research Center). She now consults for libraries and government agencies, as well as large corporations and research agencies, and also produces oral histories and memoirs for/with individuals and organizations.

Gregory Cabrera ("Taking Notes, Getting Detained [Sort of]," Chapter 4; "Biting Off More Than I Can Chew," Chapter 5; and "Culture Shock," Chapter 11) is an applied anthropologist by training and professional affiliation. He received his bachelor's and master's degrees from the Department of Anthropology at San Jose State University. In 2010 and 2012, he deployed to Afghanistan as a social scientist with the Human Terrain System Project. Today, he is a contracted researcher for TRC Professional Solutions embedded with

Voice of the Customer Team at Chick-fil-A, Inc. in Atlanta, Georgia. His full bio is at www.linkedin.com/in/gregoryscabrera.

Sharon Cartwright ("Broken Windows Theory," Chapter 9) is passionate about creating seamless experiences that work and delight the customer. Over the past decade, she has focused on understanding the user experience through research. In particular, Sharon has spent many hours observing customers interact with a range of technologies in many different environments (some requiring gumboots).

Tamara Christensen ("What the Hell? Don't You Knock?" Chapter 1) is the founder of Idea Farm. She helps organizations collaboratively solve complex business challenges by empowering cross-functional teams to learn and apply the mindset and toolset of design thinking. More about Tamara at http://ideafarmcoop.com and www.linkedin .com/in/tamarachristensen.

Patricia Colley ("The Hidden Persuader," Chapter 2) is principal at Creative Catalysts. Patricia was always a weird kid. From a very early age, she loved doing research, figuring things out, and solving difficult puzzles. Today, she specializes in deep-structure research, strategy, and design. Over the past two decades, she's worked with hundreds of clients, from mom-and-pops to Fortune 500 brands. Patricia is especially good at performing qualitative and guerrilla research, and synthesizing all sorts of random findings into coherent strategy and design work. Based in Portland, OR, with clients worldwide, Patricia's firm Creative Catalysts is a full-stack UX strategic consultancy that also offers training in creative collaboration and rapid design-thinking methods. Learn more at www.creative-catalysts.com.

Doug Cooke ("Knock-Knock! Who's There?" Chapter 2) is the founder of Tinder. A researcher with a designer's ability to visualize, Doug focuses on contextual research and integrating brand, technology, and market perspectives to create meaningful product innovation for his customers. Delivering a unique ability to bridge the gap between research findings and concepts, Doug helps clients *see* the answer instead of just reading it. With over 20 years of consulting experience, Doug has provided strategic design research and strategy services on a broad range of innovation programs for clients such as Whirlpool, Lenovo, Nestle, Logitech, and Samsung. His achievements in research and product planning have earned him recognition in the form of IDSA awards, as well as design patents.

Ryan DeGorter ("Enthusiasticus Interruptus," Chapter 3) is a UX researcher and designer in Ottawa, Canada. Ryan brings with him a background in computer science and business enabling him to tackle design problems from a variety of angles. Ryan has been in the industry for over seven years, and loves to apply UX to solve strategic initiatives. In his spare time, he can be found working with his Samoyed or biking in the Ottawa region.

Alicia Dornadic ("Don't Hate on a Tinkler," Chapter 1) is a design researcher with a background in anthropology and art history. Her current projects involve information systems, mobile technology, work organization, and more. Her blog is http://spikedpunchbowl.com and for art-related info she's @adorndesign on Instagram.

Jenn Downs ("Burns, Bandages, and BBQ," Chapter 1) is a UX designer and adores the web and what it can do for the world. She got her start in tech as MailChimp's first support rep, earning a coveted one-digit employee number of "4." She worked to grow professionally as MailChimp grew exponentially and eventually found her web calling in UX. Jenn is a mentor for Code for America and invented the slightly awkward, yet truly helpful, Laptop Hugging Method for remote mobile testing. Outside of being a web nerd, Jenn dotes on her dogs Dickie and Waylon, is a songwriter, and plays bass and sings in Atlanta bands "The Sunset District" and "The Downs." More about Jenn at www.beparticular.com.

Lisa Aronson Fitch ("When Rapport Goes Too Far," Chapter 8) is a qualitative researcher with experience in the consumer, finance, and medical fields. As a leader, her big-picture thinking style, influential voice, infectious energy, and creative insights guide business strategy and product road maps. In addition, her work guides the development of individual products with both hardware and software components. She has been proven to be instrumental in front-end innovation and often is a mentor to colleagues and project teams.

Lisa uses her qualitative research skills to develop tools and exercises for data collection. She conducts fieldwork using a variety of methods including observation, ethnography, focus groups, and in-home interviews, as well as analyzing findings to discover user needs and opportunity areas for product innovation.

Leo Frishberg ("No, We Really Meant the User," Chapter 2) is co-author of *Presumptive Design: Design Provocations for Innovation* (Morgan Kaufmann 2016) and principal of Phase II, a UX and product strategy and visioning firm based in Portland, OR (www.phaseiidesign.com). A naturalized citizen of Oregon, Frishberg and his family have called Portland home for almost 24 years. Prior to restarting Phase II, Frishberg was product design manager at Intel Corporation. A serial entrepreneur, Frishberg has started both wildly successful and disastrous businesses. He holds a BA in Environmental Planning from UCSC and a M.Arch from SCI-ARC. (Leo is Nancy's brother.)

Nancy Frishberg ("Look Sharp," Chapter 9). With a PhD in modern linguistics, Nancy brings an understanding of people—their language, culture, and context—to designing products and processes. Seeking rich responses to "why" and "how" questions, she's ready to apply a variety of qualitative methods (fieldwork, games, interviews, observation) to gauge customer satisfaction and gain user feedback. More about Nancy at www.fishbird.com and www.linkedin.com/in/nfrishberg. (Nancy is Leo's sister.)

Elaine Fukuda ("They Call Me Mister," Chapter 3) is an independent UX and design research consultant from California. More about Elaine at www.linkedin.com/in/efukuda.

Gerry Gaffney ("Right to Be Wrong," Chapter 2) runs a UX consultancy, Information and Design, in Melbourne, Australia. He also produces the popular *User Experience* podcast (http://uxpod.com). He gets some of Steve Portigal's puns, but many go over his head. On Twitter, he's @gerrygaffney.

Michael B. Griffiths, PhD ("All About Face [Sichuan Adventures]," Chapter 8) is a global expert of cultural insight and strategy at TNS.

Marta Guy ("On Confronting Judgment," Chapter 11) plays the roles of design researcher, innovation project manager, design thinking coach, world traveler, and sometime photographer at Doblin in London.

Whitney Hess ("Stories of War," Chapter 10) is an empathy and leadership coach. Find out more at https://whitneyhess.com and @whitneyhess on Twitter.

David Hoard ("Footloose," Chapter 4) is the director of product and experience design for life science instruments and software at Thermo Fisher Scientific. He is a designer by training, so he has always been in a supporter/observer role during field research. He believes that the best source of product and service innovation is in observational research and interviews, and he works to convince others of that, too.

Fumiko Ichikawa ("Good-bye, Cruel World," Chapter 9) has received her master's degree in Human Computer Interaction. In her commercial career, she has worked with many leading companies and design offices, where she took the lead in global design research. After the financial crisis and the great earthquake that took place in Northern Japan in 2011, Fumiko co-founded a company Re:public, Inc. Together with national and regional governments, companies of all sizes, and educational institutes, her mission is to empower individuals and develop innovation platforms for a better future. Fumiko is a member of Reach, the global design research network, and a founding director of Innovators 100, an innovation program commissioned by Hiroshima prefecture.

Jen Ignacz ("Bad News Turns to Couples Therapy," Chapter 10) is a UX researcher at Topp in Malmö, Sweden.

Jon Innes ("Beware of Trapdoors," Chapter 4). Despite the view that talking to users only leads to the "faster horse," Jon pioneered ethnographic methods at Oracle in the 1990s, helping to invent technology critical to eCommerce (U.S. PAT# 7181420). Using similar methods, he helped Cisco launch its highly successful VoIP phone. He then spent the next decade helping companies start and manage UX teams at places like Siebel and Intuit. He strongly believes that if your job involves improving anything, and you can't measure your impact, you should be fired. He currently runs UX Innovation LLC, a product design management consulting firm where he still peers over the shoulders of users regularly. He can be found at www.linkedin.com/in/jinnes and at @innes_jon on Twitter.

Jen Iudice ("Trust Your Gut, It Can Save Your Life!" Chapter 8) is a senior design researcher at Teague in Seattle. Jen conducts research that guides and informs Teague's design process. Jen's extensive education includes a Communication degree focused on Media Production from Alfred University in New York, coursework in strategic design planning and design research at the Institute of Design, and coursework in anthropology at the University of Chicago. Outside of work, she is an avid traveler and arts and music enthusiast. Given that her job is all about finding the big "aha" moment through research and discovery, it should come as no surprise that her lifelong goal is to "never stop learning."

Gavin Johnston ("It's 4:00 a.m. Do You Know Where Your Ethnographer Is?" Chapter 8). No stranger to the process of bringing brands to life, Gavin has over 19 years of brand consulting, strategic planning, consumer research, and design experience. His primary experience has been in pharma, finance, and CPG, but his professional reach extends far beyond his day job. He also writes a blog called "anthrostrategist" and has spoken at TEDx, GlobalShop, EPIC, POPAI, and Peeps Forum on how to create successful brands and connect deeply with audiences.

Prasad Kantamneni ("Skin in the Game," Chapter 5) is the CEO of UXReactor and manages the UXD Academy - Design School in India, with a vision of creating Best of Breed design experiences and talent in India. Prior to UXReactor, he worked for 20+ years with cutting-edge companies such as Yahoo! and Honeywell. While at Yahoo! he was the principal architect of the eye-tracking platform and was responsible for significant user experience and revenue improvements. One of the achievements he is most proud of is using research to build a case and drive the launch of the search assistance feature (also known as *search suggestions*) at Yahoo! This helped Yahoo! become the first search engine to deploy the Search Assistance feature—a feature that touches almost every Internet user today.

Dak Kopec, PhD ("Managing Biases in Research," Chapter 11) is an architectural psychologist and director of the Master of Design Studies in Design for Human Health at the Boston Architectural College. He has authored three books and co-edited a fourth. He served two terms as a Fulbright reviewer, was appointed by the Governor of Hawaii to the Health and Planning Council, delivered a TEDx talk about the importance of including nature into education, and has discussed the role of design and health in Doha, Qatar; San José, Costa Rica; and Taipei, Taiwan.

Apala Lahiri Chavan ("Whose Side Is the Researcher On?" Chapter 9) is the chief design and delivery officer at Human Factors International. Her passion is to envision how user experience changes across time and space. She has developed a vast array of user research techniques that adapt to diverse cultural and economic environments, and she specializes in creating breakthrough user experience (UX) strategy. Apala is an award-winning designer (International Audi Design Award 1996). She co-edited the book *Innovative Solutions: What Designers Need to Know for Today's Emerging Markets* and her TEDx talk is *Three Laws of User Experience*. Follow her on Twitter at @FuturistApala.

Daria Loi, BArch, PhD ("Researcher Thresholds," Chapter 2) is a principal engineer at Intel Corporation, where she drives UX innovation in the client computing group. She has been a participatory design and user experience specialist for over 18 years, has conducted UX research in most continents, published extensively, and serves as chair or committee member on a number of journals, institutes and conferences. See more at www.darialoi.com and www.linkedin.com/in/darialoi.

Diane Loviglio ("Interrupted Interview," Chapter 3) is the CEO of Boon + Gable, a mobile app that sends a personal stylist to your home. Prior to starting her second start-up, she was Mozilla's first qualitative user researcher. This war story and others were from her time at Mozilla. You can see some of her other studies and start-ups at www.dianeloviglio.com.

Jon McNeill ("Of Speed and Strip Clubs," Chapter 8). After cutting his teeth in academia exploring reflexive representations of one's culture in ethnodocumentary film (yawn!), he went into applied anthropology, ostensibly working for product development and brand research firms in Portland and LA. What he was really doing was learning to be "just one of the girls" while shopping with teens in Boston, plotting out the future of video games with ebullient Parisian gamers, and debating the finer points of political discourse with septuagenarian corn farmer bloggers in Iowa. He founded Hunter in 2010 because finding new angles to view the familiar has always driven him, and he has a passion to share that with his clients. He loves what he does because no matter the subject—from cars to carpet—every study eventually gets down to exploring the same basic human truths—like why we feel and behave the way we do—and applying these truths to the specific business issues at hand. He thinks that's endlessly exciting stuff.

Lindsay Moore ("Sexism in the City," Chapter 8) is a user experience researcher at Google in Boulder, CO, where she helps designers, engineers, and product folks develop empathy for and understanding of the people we call *users*. She worked previously at MapQuest, as an independent consultant for early-stage start-ups, and also worked in the trenches of the agency world. She does, in fact, know a bit about finance, and she hates the word *blouses*. See more at www.linkedin .com/in/lindsmoore.

Erik Moses ("[Don't] Go Toward the Light," Chapter 4) is a senior design manager at Product Development Technologies (PDT) in Lake Zurich, IL.

Debbie Mrazek ("Sometimes Ignorance Is Bliss," Chapter 6) is a design strategy and management consultant, working with both for-profit and non-profit organizations. Prior to November 2012, Deb led an international team of design strategists within HP focused on maximizing design contributions to both HP's customers and HP. Deb has been an internal consultant to HP managers around the world—developing customer-centered innovations, strategies, business models, organization designs, plans, roles, processes, and tools; a strategic planner; an experience design manager; and an experience designer. She has a Masters of Engineering, Human Factors, from Arizona State University and a Bachelor of Science, Systems Engineering and Human Factors from the University of Illinois.

Andrew Muir Wood ("Victims of the Killer Insight," Chapter 7). Before building his customer insights team at DueDil in London, Andrew worked as a design strategy consultant for global consumer technology clients and then started his own design research consultancy for start-ups. He is a UX research mentor at Google Launchpad and also works on initiatives and events for young creatives and entrepreneurs around the UK. He is on Twitter at @muirwd.

Ari Nave ("Chicken Run," Chapter 4) is a design anthropologist living in the Bay Area with his wife and three kids, Sagan, Win, and Theory. He leverages evolutionary psychology to help define the design of products, service, and experiences through The King's Indian, Inc. This work includes the proactive design of corporate cultures that spread to dominate an organization. He is also exploring changes to masculinity through http://letter25.com and working on a documentary, *Y*, on personal journeys of fatherhood and masculinity.

Dennis Nordstrom ("Negotiating Between Sympathy and Empathy," Chapter 5) is a design researcher who has spent the last 10 years thinking about strategy and design, and who has applied his experience with both of those to create products that aim at improving people's lives. Dennis has had the good fortune of pursuing his passion for design thinking in Denmark, Australia, and now in the United States, where he has worked on projects concerning finance, travel, health care, and local search. Currently, Dennis works at Edmunds.com, where he is acting as a resident UX researcher. In this role, Dennis will interview car shoppers and car dealers to bridge the transactional divide between shoppers and dealers. This is done by utilizing design thinking to create services that help alleviate some of the pain points that are often experienced within the sales process of cars.

Nicolas Nova ("Do You Want Me to Act?" Chapter 3) is co-founder and ethnographer at the Near Future Laboratory.

Vanessa Pfafflin ("DDoSed in Vegas," Chapter 3) is a user experience researcher at Hired in San Francisco.

Ilona Posner ("First Stop the Bleeding!" Chapter 9) has been working in user experience for over 25 years, since before the field was called *user experience*. She has consulted for corporations and start-ups, in different industries including telecom, technology, finance, health care, and transportation. Ilona enjoys tackling different challenges including user research, user-centered design, digital strategy, and training. As an experienced and dedicated educator, she has been teaching user experience since 2000 and has taught hundreds of students at universities (University of Toronto, OCAD University, and Media Lab at the Canadian Film Centre) and industries (HFI, Rogers, CIBC, Deutsche Bank, Scotiabank). Ilona holds a master's degree in Computer Science from the University of Toronto, so she can speak to developers. She has three grown children and elderly parents who serve both as cultural ambassadors and as constant reminders about differences among users and their experiences. See more at www. ilonaposner.com.

George Ressler ("Skyfall [or A View to a Kill]," Chapter 1). Growing up, George was always getting his hands dirty. He enjoyed the process of building things and was constantly constructing, whether it was inventive backyard forts or intricate Lego masterpieces. George's hunger for creation led him to study industrial design at the University of Kansas, where he eventually discovered his passion for design research. Today, George utilizes his dual design and research background to understand the needs of users and connect those insights to clients' business strategies. He has over five years of experience working as a design research and strategy consultant for clients across multiple industries, including Chrysler, GE Healthcare, Johnson & Johnson, Nationwide Insurance, and Kohler. George is passionate about people. He enjoys design research because it regularly exposes him to new people, environments, and problems. An enthusiastic advocate for end users, George loves that design research's combination of impact and scale allows him to truly make a difference in people's lives. See more at www.georgeressler.com and @georgeressler on Twitter.

Carol Rossi ("Driving Force," Chapter 6) is the senior director of user experience research at Edmunds where she's led the research effort since 2010. Her approach is to uncover insights through deep listening and acute observation, whether she's observing face-to-face or looking at data, and then connect the dots to help product and marketing teams create something meaningful. With 20+ years of experience, she's led projects around vision and strategy setting, brand retention, and building, as well as tactical UX research. For a dozen years, she taught yoga, and she loves art, dance, design, and fashion. She has M.A. degrees in Human Factors and Dance Ethnology. See more at www.linkedin.com/in/crossiux and @crossiUX on Twitter. Listen to the *Dollars to Donuts* podcast at www.portigal.com/podcast/6-carol-rossi-of-edmunds-com/.

Raffaella Roviglioni ("Learning to Deal with Expectations," Chapter 11). A UX researcher and designer since 2009, Raffaella has a scientific background in agriculture and told her story about moving toward UX at EuroIA. She is based in Rome, Italy, working as a freelance consultant on national and international projects dealing with user research, usability testing, UX design, co-design, and facilitation. She is a partner at Usertestlab and UX Fellows networks. Raffaella is also a trainer and teacher on UX strategy, design, and research. Together with Alessio Ricco, she developed a workshop format, Improv.e UX using improv games for developing better soft skills (www.improveux.it). See more at https://it.linkedin.com/in/raffiro and @raffiro on Twitter.

Sean Ryan ("Pockets Full of Cash," Chapter 1) has been a practicing ethnographer for the past 17 years, including consulting work, a short stint at Staples, and the past 11 years at Bose Corporation. In the age of diminishing attention spans, he has started to focus more on crafting high-quality video stories to highlight his ethnographic work. Sean is fond of food, film, travel, and aggressive racquetball playing.

Brandon Satanek ("CATastrophe," Chapter 5) is a UX manager, designer, and researcher in corporate America. He occasionally blogs about experience design with a nod to Disney parks at http:// EXPERIENCEdzine.com and is @BrandonSatanek on Twitter.

Steve Sato ("Finding Mojo in the Moment," Conclusion) was the founder of Sato + Partners, a firm that worked with executives of experience design and innovation to help them more successfully promote, position, practice, and produce customer-driven innovations. Steve's passion was in helping executives successfully position and promote key innovation, design, and experience initiatives, in order to build sustained "design/integrative thinking" capability, customer-centered business strategy and planning. Steve held a Master of Design from the Institute of Design at Illinois Institute of Technology, a Master of Engineering Management from Northwestern University and a Bachelor of Science, Mechanical Engineering, from the University of Illinois. Steve's passion for fly fishing and the outdoors is what drew him, his wife Dixie, and their Portuguese Water Dogs to the Pacific Northwest.

Rachel Shadoan ("Research, in Sickness and in Health," Chapter 9) is the co-founder and CEO of Akashic Labs, a Portland-based research and development consultancy, where she specializes in combining research methodologies to provide rich and accurate answers to pressing questions. Prior to founding Akashic Labs, she worked with Intel exploring both how people use their phones in cars and how the ability to convert to a tablet impacts laptop use. When she's not playing with data, she can be found optimizing her balcony for planting space and live-tweeting episodes of *Mister Rogers' Neighborhood*. See more at www.akashiclabs.com.

Susan Simon Daniels ("A Sigh Is Just a Sigh," Chapter 10). As a customer experience researcher, she listens to and observes people, but not in a creepy way. In her pursuit to make things easier to use, she searches for truths universally acknowledged. She is a random quoter of poetry and a proud member of Red Sox nation. Visit https://ca.linkedin.com/in/ssimondaniels for the professional stuff.

Priya Sohoni ("Taking Empathy to a Whole New Level," Chapter 11) is an architect turned product designer turned user researcher—and still passionate about all of those things. She's spent the last 14 years interviewing people around the world for all kinds of topics—breakfast habits of semiprofessional athletes, feminine hygiene in different cultures, end-of-life wishes of dying people, fast food drive-thru packaging, and small business mobile apps. Listening to people's stories and developing a deep empathy for who they are, and why they do what they do, keeps her energized. Nowadays, you'll find her working at SAP Labs, Palo Alto, as well as teaching at universities around the Bay Area.

Dan Soltzberg ("Focus, No Matter What!" Chapter 9) is a design lead and design research community lead at IDEO. An avid photographer and observer of patterns, he blogs (sporadically) at www.strikeanywhereinsights.wordpress.com.

Mary Ann Sprague ("Be Prepared," Chapter 1) is a user experience ethnographer at Palo Alto Research Center in Webster, NY, and has been with Xerox since 1985. Over her career, she has worked on copier product development, user interface architecture, tools, and development, as well as network scanning and accounting architectures. Past ethnographic studies have looked at technical publishing, production, digital color and transactional printing, the future of work, education, and service operations. See more at www.linkedin.com/in/mary-ann-sprague-533b425.

Cordy Swope ("A Crisis of Credibility," Chapter 2) is senior director at Johnson & Johnson Design. He leads a team of service designers, design researchers, and strategists called *Insights and Experience Strategy* (IXS) whose remit is to use design thinking to open up innovative new ways of delivering health care across multiple sectors—from consumer products to advanced systems and business models. Prior to J&J, Cordy led interdisciplinary groups at IDEO, Fahrenheit 212, and Continuum in creating new offerings for various clients, in different industries. Along the way, his teams developed many foundational design-thinking methodologies, eventually bringing them to bear on organizational transformation and culture change initiatives—thus, helping many global Fortune 500 companies become more innovative. His past clients include BASF, BMW, Eli Lilly, GE Capital, Gaggenau, Herman Miller, Nokia, Orange, P&G, Mercedes, Novartis, Renault, Siemens, Telefónica, and Vaillant. His work has won design awards and has also appeared in the Museum of Modern Art, New York.

Dan Szuc ("Shanghai Surprise," Chapter 1) is a co-founder and principal at Apogee and co-founder of Make Meaningful Work, as well as the co-founder of UX Hong Kong. He has been involved in the UX field for over 20 years, and has been based in Hong Kong for over 20 years. Dan has lectured about user-centered design globally. He has co-authored two books including *Global UX* with Whitney Quesenbery and the *Usability Kit* with Gerry Gaffney. He is @dszuc on Twitter.

Julia Thompson ("For Want of a Shoe," Chapter 1). Beginning with a bachelor's degree in Industrial Design, she quickly discovered that her creativity and inspiration came from understanding user needs. This realization led her to pursue a career in design research where she applies the following principles:

- I believe users should be heard. I believe their experiences can ignite innovation, can ground decision-making, and can provide valuable input into the design process.

- In my work, I facilitate bringing the stories, behaviors, and opinions of users to the companies whose products they use—to the creative minds and to the decision-makers alike.

- I do this by conducting primary research through interviews and in-context observation to identify patterns, pain points, and opportunity areas.

See more at https://ca.linkedin.com/in/juliamthompson.

Jen Van Riet ("Jennie's Got a Gun," Chapter 8) is a freelance user experience researcher living in Carlsbad, CA. She holds a PhD in Cognitive Psychology from the University of California, Riverside. Since 2001, Jen has been providing user research services for companies, including Intuit, Microsoft, Yahoo!, America Online, and NCR among others. In 2010, Jen was trained as a design thinking coach (aka innovation catalyst) and since then has been helping teams gain deep customer empathy, go broad in their design ideas, and test ideas rapidly.

Susan Wilhite ("The Trust Dance," Chapter 7) is an ethnographer in the San Francisco Bay Area. Her generative and formative research has shaped new brand-expanding products and services at Google, Samsung, Microsoft, and Kaiser Permanente. She also performs occasional live stand-up storytelling. Susan has a BA in Anthropology from the University of New Mexico, a MA in Anthropology from UCLA, and accreditation in healthcare built environment research (EDAC).

Anne Williams ("Emotions at Work: What We Can Learn from a Psychiatric Case Manager," Chapter 10) is a case manager in the department of inpatient psychiatry at Kaiser Permanente. (Anne is Tom's sister.)

Tom Williams ("Go with the Flow," Chapter 8) is an ethnographer and a co-founder of Point Forward, an innovation strategy consulting firm. He has conducted hundreds of interviews in a variety of settings across 12 countries. (Tom is Anne's brother.)

Chauncey Wilson ("Secrets, Security, and Contextual Inquiry," Chapter 4) is a user experience consultant and retired adjunct professor at Bentley University. He has presented often at UXPA, STC, CHI, APA, IxDA, and HFES conferences. Chauncey has published many books, chapters, and articles on usability engineering, brainstorming, surveys, and research and design methods. He enjoys the roles of mentor and "chief skeptic." Chauncey was a recipient of the 2015 UXPA Lifetime Achievement Award.

Rachel Wong ("Subject Matter May Be Inappropriate," Chapter 6) is a design researcher and founder of How We Meet (http://howwemeet.net), a research and storytelling consultancy. She earned her research chops working within prominent design agencies and consumer product companies. Over the years, she's spanned the globe, researching topics as varied as energy bars, the plight of the unemployed, and smart television interfaces. Rachel's side interests include radio storytelling and fiction writing.

ACKNOWLEDGMENTS

A book of stories wouldn't exist without storytellers. Beyond the storytellers in this book, I've talked to many people over the years about their experiences in the field. Those stories—fully fleshed-out or mere nubbins—have fueled my excitement to gather, reflect on, and share what really goes down in fieldwork. Many researchers contributed stories, both here and to the online archive. The authors included in this book went the extra distance—signing documents, climbing into attics to find old photos, writing bios, filling out online forms, and other annoying but helpful tasks.

In addition to the stories themselves, I benefited a great deal from people who helped with this book and with everything that led to the idea of this becoming a book. Dak Kopec, David Bloxsom, and Anne Willams agreed to provide their enlightening perspectives from outside the user research domain. Irene Au, Marc Hébert, Shana Hughes, Dan Olsen, Celeste Roschuni, Steve Sanderson, Gabe Trionfi, and Tom Williams reviewed early drafts and offered encouragement, challenges, and additions. Marc Hébert, Shana Hughes, Tom Williams, Sally Steuer, and Anne Williams (my partner, who supports me in absolutely everything) put time and passion into brainstorming the vision and mission of this book.

Tammy Sachs, Whitney Quesenbery, Miles Begin, John Payne, Kelly Braun, Diane Loviglio, Carla Borsoi, Tom Williams, Doug Cooke, Jon McNeil, Steve Sato, Rachel Shadoan, Jennifer Pretti, Julia Thompson, and Susan Simon Daniels all told war stories, live, at various events. The organizers of CHIFOO, UX Australia, and Fluxible invited me to talk about war stories to their audiences.

As soon as the stories began to appear online, Cat Macaulay began using them with her students. Susan Dray wrote a lovely piece for Core77 about the power of these stories. Christina Wodtke offered guidance on stories and storytelling.

Marta Justak and Lou Rosenfeld encouraged and challenged me in working out just what this book could and should be. It's been a particular joy to get to work with them again. Karen Corbett and Stephanie Zhong facilitated dozens of small and large pieces of the process.

I am tremendously grateful to all of these people.

ABOUT THE AUTHOR

Steve Portigal helps companies think and act strategically when innovating with user insights. He has led organizations of all types to align around a fresh understanding of their users. Out in the field, he has interviewed families eating breakfast, hotel maintenance staff, architects, rock musicians, home-automation enthusiasts, credit-default swap traders, and radiologists.

Steve speaks regularly at corporate events and conferences such as Confab, Fluxible, Interaction, SXSW, UX Australia, UX Hong Kong, UX Lisbon, and UX New Zealand. He is the author of the now-classic book *Interviewing Users* and host of the *Dollars to Donuts* podcast.

Steve built one of the first online communities (Undercover, a Rolling Stones fan group) in 1992, nurturing it from a time when the Internet was an underground academic technology through to today.

After growing up near Toronto, Steve eventually made his way to the San Francisco Bay Area where he's been for more than 20 years. He lives in the coastal town of Montara with his partner Anne and their exuberant dog Buster. Steve loves to travel and eat interesting food and to take pictures of travel and interesting food. He also really loves to nap.